محمد رسول الله

Muhammad
The Messenger of Allah

May Allah Exalt his Mention

© Abdurahman Abdulkarim Al–Sheha , 2005

King Fahd National Library Cataloging -in-Publication Data

Al-Sheha, Abdulrahman

Muhammad : The Messenger of islam. / Abdulrahman

Al-Sheha – Riyadh . 2005

P : 98 C M : 14 X 21

ISBN : 9960-47-364-3

1- Prophet Muhammad life   1-Title

239 dc   1426/626

L.D. no. 1426/626

ISBN : 9960-47-364-3

محمد رسول الله

Muhammad
The Messenger of Allah

May Allah Exalt his Mention

Written by:
Abdurrahman al-Sheha

Translated by:
Abdurrahmaan Murad

إصدار :

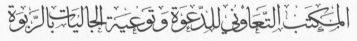

الربوة - شارع الأمير متعب (الأربعين) - خلف فرع شركة الراجحي المصرفية للاستثمار
ص. ب: 29465 الرياض 11457 - هاتف 4454900 - 4916065 - ناسوخ 4970126
P.O.BOX 29465 ARRIYADH 11457 - TEL 4454900 - 4916065
FAX 4970126 - e-mail: rabwah@islamhouse.com
http://www.islamhouse.com

طبع على نفقة مركز توعية الجاليات بالقصيم
هاتف 3248980 - 06/3243100 فاكس 06/3245414
أرقام الحساب العام للمركز
مصرف الراجحي 10860101094158 - البنك الأهلي 3915424100000201

Terminology used in this Book

(Taken from Sheik Mahmoud Murad's book *'Common mistakes in Translation'*)

1. ***Rubb***: Some prefer to translate the term *'Rubb'* into 'Lord.' Beside the fact that the latter is a Biblical term referring to the alleged lordship of the slave of Allah, Prophet Jesus, the word 'lord' which is limited to 'master', 'chief', 'proprietor', or 'ruler', can never convey the conclusive signification of the term *'Rubb'*. Among other signification, the term *'Rubb'* means, the Creator, the Fashioner, the Provider, the One upon Whom all creatures depend for their means of subsistence, and the One Who gives life and causes death.

2. ***Deen***: The word translated as religion is *'Deen'*, which in Arabic commonly refers to a way of life, which is both private and public. It is an inclusive term meaning: acts of worship, political practice, and a detailed code of conduct, including hygiene or etiquette matters.

3. [🕌] ***Sal'lal'laahu a'laihi wa sal'lam.*** Some translate it as 'peace be upon him'. This translation is incorrect; the correct translation is, 'may Allah exalt his mention, and render him and his household safe and secure from every derogatory thing'.

All praise is due to Allah, the *Rubb* of the worlds, and may Allah exalt the mention of His Prophet, and render him and his household safe and secure from all derogatory things.

When talking about Prophet Muhammad 🕌 one should keep in mind that he is talking about the greatest individual in history. This is not a baseless claim; for the one who reads his biography, and learns of his mannerisms and ethics, while keeping aside all preconceived notions would certainly reach this conclusion. Some fair and just non-Muslims have reached this conclusion as well.

Professor Hasan Ali, may Allah have mercy on him, said in his magazine *'Noor al-Islam'* that a Brahmin[1] colleague of his once told him: 'I recognize and believe that the Messenger of Islam is the greatest and most mature man in history.' Professor Hasan Ali, may Allah have mercy on him, asked him: 'Why do you consider him as the greatest and most mature man?' He answered: 'No man possessed the characteristics, mannerisms and ethics that he possessed at one time. He was a king under whom the entire peninsula was unified; yet he was humble. He believed that the dominion belonged to his God alone.

Great riches would come to him, and yet he lived in a state of poverty; fire would not be lit in his house for many days and he would stay hungry. He was a great leader; he led small numbers into battle against thousands, and yet he would decisively defeat them. He loved peace agreements, and would agree to them with a firm heart; even though he had thousands

---

[1] Brahmin: member of the highest of the four Hindu castes: the priestly caste.

of his brave and courageous Companions by his side. Each Companion was very brave and could confront a thousand enemies alone, while not feeling the least bit intimidated. Yet, the Prophet was kind-hearted, merciful, and did not want to shed a drop of blood. He was deeply concerned about the affairs of the Arabian Peninsula, yet he did not neglect the affairs of his family, household, or the poor and needy. He was keen to disseminate Islam amongst those who had gone astray. In general, he was a man concerned with the betterment and wellbeing of mankind, yet he did not indulge in amassing worldly fortune. He busied himself with the worship of Allah and loved doings deeds which pleased Allah. He never avenged himself on account of personal reasons. He even prayed for his enemies' wellbeing, and would warn them of the punishment of Allah.

He was an ascetic regarding worldly affairs and would worship Allah throughout the night. He was the brave and courageous soldier who fought with the sword - and the infallible Prophet - the conqueror who conquered nations and countries. He slept on a mat of hay, and a pillow filled with coarse fibers. People crowned him as the Sultan over Arabs, or King of the Arabian Peninsula, yet his family lived a simple life, even after they received great fortunes; the riches were piled in the Masjid. Fatima complained to him about the strenuous work she did, the grinding stone and water jug which she used to carry - how they had left marks on her body. The Messenger at that time was dividing the female and male slaves amongst the Muslims. He did not give her a portion of that wealth; instead, the Prophet taught her a few words and supplications. His Companion, Umar came to his house and looked in his room, and saw nothing but a hay mat which the Prophet was sitting on, which had left marks on his body. The only provisions in the house were half a *Saa'* (measure of weight) of barley in a container, and a water skin that hung on the wall - this is all the Messenger of Allah owned at a time half the Arabs were under his control. When Umar saw this, he could not control himself and wept. The Messenger of Allah 🕊 said: 'Why are you weeping O Umar?' He replied: 'Why shouldn't I weep - Khosrau and Caesar enjoy themselves in this world and the Messenger of Allah 🕊 only owns what I see!' He responded: 'O Umar, wouldn't it please you that this is the share of Khosrau and Caesar in this life, and in the Hereafter this pleasure would be for us alone?'

When the Prophet examined his troops prior to the occupation of Makkah, Abu Sufyan stood beside al-Ab'bas, the uncle of the Prophet 🕊 and they looked at the banners of the Muslim army. Abu Sufyan at that time was not a Muslim. He was amazed by the vast number of Muslims; they advanced towards Makkah like a torrent of water. No one could stop them and nothing stood in their way. Abu Sufyan then said to al-Ab'bas: 'O Ab'bas, your nephew has become a grand King!' Ab'bas responded saying: 'This is not kingship, rather prophethood, and the Message of Islam.'

Ad'ee at-Ta'ee, the son of Ha'tim at-Ta'ee who is the paradigm of generosity, attended the assembly of the Prophet 🕊 while he was still a Christian. When he saw how the Companions aggrandized and respected the Prophet, he was confused - was he a Prophet or a king? He asked himself, 'is this a king or a Messenger of the Messengers of Allah?' While he was pondering over this, a destitute woman came to the Prophet 🕊 and said: 'I wish to tell you a secret.' He said to her: 'which road in Madinah do you want me to meet you in?' The Prophet 🕊

left with the destitute maid, and took care of her needs. When Ad'ee saw the humbleness of the Prophet, he realized the truth and discarded the crosses that he was wearing and became a Muslim.'

We will mention some statements of the Orientalists concerning Muhammad 🕊. We as Muslims believe in the Prophet 🕊 and his Message. We are mentioning these statements for the following two reasons:

a. To serve as a reminder and admonition for name-sake Muslims who abandoned their Prophet, so that they would heed and return to their *Deen*.

b. So that non-Muslims would know who the Prophet is from the statements of their own people, so that they would be guided to Islam.

I ask these people to not hold any preconceived notions when searching for the truth, when reading this or any other Islamic material. I ask Allah to open their hearts and chests to accept the truth, and to show them the right path and inspire them to follow it.

Abdurrahmaan b. Abdul-Kareem al-Sheha

Riyadh, 11535

P.O. Box 59565

Email: alsheha@yahoo.com

http://www.islamland.org

Who is the Messenger, Muhammad 🕮?

His Lineage:

He is Abul-Qasim (father of Al-Qasim) Muhammad, son of Abdullah, son of Abdul-Mutalib. His lineage traces back to the tribe of Adnan, son of Ismael [the Prophet of Allah, the son of Ibraheem, the one whom Allah chose for His love] may Allah exalt their mention. His mother is Aminah, daughter of Wahb.

The Prophet 🕮 said:

> 'Indeed Allah chose the tribe of Kinanah over other tribes from the children of Ismail; He chose the Quraish over other tribes of Kinanah; He chose Banu Hashim over the other families of the Quraish; and He chose me from Banu Hashim.' (Muslim #2276)

Thus, the Prophet 🕮 has the noblest lineage on earth. His enemies attested to this fact; Abu Sufyan, who was the arch enemy of Islam before he became Muslim, attested to this fact in front of Heraclius, the Ruler of Rome.

Abdullah b. Ab'bas, with whom Allah is pleased, reported that the Messenger of Allah 🕮 wrote to Caesar and invited him to Islam and sent him a letter with Dihya Al-Kalbi, who handed it to the Governor of Busra who then forwarded it to Caesar.

Caesar as a sign of gratitude to Allah, had walked from *Hims* to *Ilya* (i.e. Jerusalem) when Allah had granted Him victory over the Persian forces. So, when the letter of the Messenger of Allah reached Caesar, he said after reading it, **"Seek for me anyone of his people,** (Arabs of Quraish tribe) **if present here, in order to ask him about the Messenger of Allah!"** At that time Abu Sufyan bin Harb was in Sham with some men from Quraish who had come (to Sham) as merchants during the truce that had been concluded between the Messenger of Allah; and the infidels of Quraish. Abu Sufyan said, **'Caesar's messenger found us somewhere in Sham so he took me and my companions to** *Ilya* **and we were admitted into Caesar's presence to find him sitting in his royal court wearing a crown and surrounded by the senior Byzantine dignitaries. He said to his translator. "Ask them whom amongst them is a close relation to the man who claims to be a prophet."'**

Abu Sufyan added, 'I replied: "I am the nearest relative to him." He asked, "What degree of relationship do you have with him?" I replied, "He is my cousin," and there was none of *Bani Abd Manaf* in the caravan except myself. Caesar said, "Let him come nearer." He then ordered that my companions stand behind me near my shoulder and said to his translator, "Tell his companions that I am going to ask this man about the man who claims to be a prophet. If he tells a lie, they should contradict him immediately."'

Abu Sufyan added, 'By Allah! Had it not been for shame that my companions brand me a liar, I would not have spoken the truth about him when he asked me. But I considered it shameful to be called a liar by my companions, so I told the truth.'

'He then said to his translator, "Ask him what kind of family he belongs to." I replied, "He belongs to a noble family amongst us." He said, "Has anybody else amongst you ever claimed the same before him?" I replied, "No." He said, "Have you ever blamed him for telling lies before he claimed what he claimed?" I replied, "No." He said, "Was anybody amongst his ancestors a king?" I replied, "No." He said, "Do the noble or the poor follow him?" I replied, 'It is the poor who follow him." He said, "Are they increasing or decreasing (daily)?" I replied, "They are increasing." He said, "Does anybody amongst those who embrace his *Deen* become displeased and then discard his *Deen*?" I replied, "No." He said, 'Does he break his promises?" I replied, "No, but we are now at truce with him and we are afraid that he may betray us."

Abu Sufyan added, 'Other than the last sentence, I could not say anything against him.'

'Caesar then asked, "Have you ever had a war with him?" I replied, "Yes." He said, "What was the outcome of your battles with him?" I replied, "Sometimes he was victorious and sometimes we." He said, "What does he order you to do?" I said, "He tells us to worship Allah alone, and not to worship others along with Him, and to leave all that our fore-fathers used to worship. He orders us to pray, give in charity, be chaste, keep promises and return what is entrusted to us. '''

'When I had said that, Caesar said to his translator, "Say to him: I asked you about his lineage and your reply was that he belonged to a noble family. In fact, all the Messengers came from the noblest lineage of their nations. Then I questioned you whether anybody else amongst you had claimed such a thing, and your reply was in the negative. If the answer had been in the affirmative, I would have thought that this man was following a claim that had been said before him. When I asked you whether he was ever blamed for telling lies, your reply was in the negative, so I took it for granted that a person who did not tell a lie to people could never tell a lie about Allah. Then I asked you whether any of his ancestors was a king. Your reply was in the negative, and if it had been in the affirmative, I would have thought that this man wanted to take back his ancestral kingdom. When I asked you whether the rich or the poor people followed him, you replied that it was the poor who followed him. In fact, such are the followers of the Messengers. Then I asked you whether his followers were increasing or decreasing. You replied that they were increasing. In fact, this is the result of true faith till it is complete (in all respects). I asked you whether there was anybody who, after embracing his *Deen*, became displeased and discarded his *Deen*; your reply was in the negative. In fact, this is the sign of true faith, for when its pleasure enters and mixes in the hearts completely; nobody will be displeased with it. I asked you whether he had ever broken his promise. You replied in the negative. And such are the Messengers; they never break their promises. When I asked you whether you fought with him and he fought with you, you replied that he did and that sometimes he was victorious and sometimes you. Indeed, such are the Messengers; they are put to trials and the final victory is always theirs. Then I asked you what he ordered you. You replied that he ordered you to worship Allah alone and not to worship others along with Him, to leave all that your fore-fathers used to worship, to offer prayers, to speak the truth, to be chaste, to keep promises, and to return what is entrusted to you. These are really the qualities of a prophet who, I knew (from the previous Scriptures) would appear, but I did not know that he would be from amongst you. If what you say is true, he will very soon occupy the earth under my feet, and if I knew that I would reach him definitely, I would go immediately to meet him; and were I with him, then I would certainly wash his feet."'

Abu Sufyan added, 'Caesar then asked for the letter of the Messenger of Allah and it was read. Its contents were:

"I begin with the name of Allah, the most Beneficent, the most Merciful (This letter is) from Muhammad, the slave of Allah, and His Messenger, to Heraclius, the Ruler of the Byzantine. Peace be upon the followers of guidance. I invite you to Islam (i.e. surrender to Allah). Accept Islam and you will be safe; accept Islam and Allah will bestow on you a double reward. But if you reject this invitation of Islam, you shall be responsible for misguiding the peasants (i.e. your nation). O people of the Scriptures! Come to a word common between you and us, that we worship Allah, and that we associate nothing in worship with Him; and that none of us shall take others as Gods besides Allah. Then if they turn away, say: Bear witness that we are they who have surrendered (unto Him)" [3.64]

Abu Sufyan added, 'When Heraclius had finished his speech, there was a great hue and cry caused by the Byzantine dignitaries surrounding him, and there was so much noise that I did not understand what they said. So, we were ordered out of the court.'

'When I went out with my companions and we were alone, I said to them, "Verily, *Ibn Abi Kabsha's* (i.e. the Prophet's) affair has gained power. This is the King of Bani Al-Asfar fearing him."'

Abu Sufyan added: 'By Allah, I became surer and surer that his *Deen* would be victorious till I ended up accepting Islam.'

(Bukhari #2782)

Place of Birth and childhood:

The Prophet 鵩 was born in the year 571 (according to the Gregorian calendar) in the tribe of Quraish [which was held noble by all Arabs] in Makkah [which was considered the religious capital of the Arabian Peninsula].

The Arabs would perform Hajj in Makkah, and circumambulate the Ka'bah which was built by Prophet Ibrahim and his son Prophet Ismael, may Allah exalt their mention.

The Prophet 鵩 was an orphan. His father passed away before he was born, and his mother died when he was six years old. His grandfather, Abdul-Mutalib, took care of him, and when he died, his uncle, Abu Talib, took care of him. His tribe and the other tribes worshipped idols made from stone, wood and even gold. Some of these idols were placed around the Ka'bah. People believed that these idols could ward-off harm or extend benefit.

The Prophet 鵩 was a trustworthy and honest person. He never behaved treacherously, nor did he lie or cheat; he was known amongst his people as *'Al-Ameen'*, or **'The Trustworthy'**. People would entrust him with their valuables when they wanted to travel. He was also known as *'As-Sadiq'* or **'The Truthful'** for he never told a lie. He was well-mannered, well-spoken, and he loved to help people. His people loved and revered him and he had beautiful manners. Allah, the Exalted, says:

❴Indeed you are of a great moral character.❵ [68:4]

Thomas Carlyle[2] said in his book: *'Heroes, Hero-Worship and the Heroic in History'*:

'But, from an early age, he had been remarked as a thoughtful man. His companions named him "*Al Amin*, The Faithful." A man of truth and fidelity; true in what he did, in what he spoke and thought. They noted that he always meant something. A man rather taciturn in speech; silent when there was nothing to be said; but pertinent, wise, sincere, when he did speak; always throwing light on the matter. This is the only sort of speech worth speaking! Through life we find him to have been regarded as an altogether solid, brotherly, genuine man. A serious, sincere character; yet amiable, cordial, companionable, jocose even - a good laugh in him withal: there are men whose laugh is as untrue as anything about them; who cannot laugh. A spontaneous, passionate, yet just, true-meaning man! Full of wild faculty, fire and light; of wild worth, all uncultured; working out his life - takes in the depth of the Desert there.'

The Prophet 靉 liked to seclude himself in the cave of *Hira* before he was commissioned as a prophet. He would stay there many nights at a time.

He 靉 did not practice falsehood; he did not drink any intoxicants, nor did he bow to a statue or idol, or take an oath by them or offer to them an offering. He was a shepherd over a flock of sheep which belonged to his people. **The Prophet** 靉 said:

'Every prophet commissioned by Allah was a shepherd over a flock of sheep.' His companions asked him: **'Even**

---

[2] He was a famous historian and writer. He was born in Ecclefechan, Scotland. He died in 1885.

you, O Messenger of Allah?' He said: 'Yes, I would take care of a flock of sheep for the people of Makkah.' (Bukhari 2143)

When Prophet Muhammad 靏 turned forty, he received divine revelation; he was at the cave of Hira. The Mother of the believers, **A'ishah**, with whom Allah is pleased, said:

'The first thing that Allah's Messenger 靏 received, while in the Cave of *Hira* in Makkah, were good visions [dreams]. Every time he had a dream, it would come true and clear, like the split of the dawn. Later on, Allah's Messenger 靏 began to love being alone in meditation. He spent lengthy periods for days and nights to fulfil this purpose in the Cave before returning back to his family. He would take a supply of food for his trip. When he came back to his wife Khadeejah, with whom Allah is pleased, he would get a fresh supply of food and go back to the same Cave to continue his meditation.'

'The Truth came to him while he was in the Cave of *Hira*. The Angel Jibreel 靏 came to Muhammad 靏 and commanded him to read. Muhammad 靏 replied: **"I cannot read!"** Jibreel 靏 embraced Muhammad 靏 until he could not breathe, and then let him go saying: **"O Muhammad! Read!"** Again, Muhammad 靏 replied: **"I cannot read!"** Jibreel 靏 embraced Muhammad 靏 for the second time. He then ordered him to read for the third time, when he did not he embraced him tightly until he could not breathe, and then let him go saying: **"O Muhammad!**

❴Recite with the Name of Your *Rubb*! Who created, Created man, out of a (mere) clot of congealed blood: Proclaim! And your *Rubb* is Most Bountiful.❵ [96:1-3]

The Messenger of Allah 靏 returned home trembling. He entered his home and told Khadeejah: **"Cover me up, cover me** up!" Khadeejah, with whom Allah is pleased, covered Muhammad 🕊 until he felt better. He then informed her about what happened to him in the Cave of *Hira*. He said, **"I was concerned about myself and my well-being."** Khadeejah, with whom Allah is pleased, assured Muhammad 🕊 saying: **"By Allah! You don't have to worry! Allah, the Exalted, will never humiliate you! You are good to your kith and kin. You help the poor and needy. You are generous and hospitable to your guests. You help people who are in need."** Khadeejah, with whom Allah is pleased, took her husband Muhammad 🕊 to a cousin of hers named Waraqah bin Nawfal bin Asad bin Abdul Uzza. This man became a Christian during the Era of Ignorance. He was a scribe, who wrote the Scripture in Hebrew. He was an old man who became blind at the latter part of his life. Khadeejah, with whom Allah is pleased, said to her cousin, **"O cousin, listen to what your nephew [i.e. Muhammad 🕊] is about to tell you!"** Waraqah said: **"What is it you have seen, dear nephew?"** The Messenger of Allah 🕊 informed him of what he had seen in the Cave of *Hira*. Upon hearing his report, Waraqah said, **"By Allah! This is the Angel Jibreel ﷺ who came to Prophet Musa ﷺ. I wish I would be alive when your people will drive you out of Makkah!"** The Messenger of Allah 🕊 wondered: **"Are they going to drive me out of Makkah?!"** Waraqah affirmed positively saying, **"Never has a man conveyed a Message similar to what you have been charged with, except that his people waged war against him - if I am to witness this, I will support you."** Waraqah lived only a short period after this incident and passed away. Revelation also stopped for a while.' (Bukhari #3)

The chapter of the Qur'an quoted in the hadeeth above marks the beginning when he was commissioned as a Prophet. **Allah**, the Exalted, then revealed to him:

《O you (Muhammad 🕌) enveloped (in garments); Arise and warn! And your *Rubb* (Allah) magnify !And your garments purify!》 (74:1-4)

This chapter of the Qur'an marks the beginning when he was commissioned as a Messenger.

With the revelation of this chapter of the Qur'an the Prophet 🕌 began calling his people to Islam openly. He began with his own people. Some of them refused adamantly to listen to him because he was calling them to a matter which they had not witnessed before.

The *Deen* of Islam is a complete way of life, which deals with religious, political, economical and social affairs. Furthermore, the *Deen* of Islam did not only call them to worship Allah alone, and to forsake all idols and things they worshipped; rather, it prohibited them from things they considered pleasurable, such as consuming interest and intoxicants, fornication, and gambling. It also called people to be just and fair with one another, and to know that there was no difference between them except through piety. How could the Quraish [the noblest tribe amongst Arabs] stand to be treated equally with the slaves!! They did not only adamantly refuse to accept Islam; rather, they harmed him and blamed him, saying that he was a crazy person, a sorcerer and a liar. They blamed him with things they would not dare to have blamed him with before the advent of Islam. They incited the ignorant masses against him, and harmed him and tortured his companions. Abdullah b. Masood, with whom Allah is pleased, said:

'While the Prophet ﷺ was standing up and praying near the Ka'bah, a group of Quraish were sitting in their sitting place, one of them said: 'Do you see this man? Would someone bring the dirt and filth and bloody intestines from the camels of so and so, and wait till he prostrates, and then place it between his shoulders? The most wretched amongst them volunteered to do it, and when the Prophet ﷺ prostrated, he put the filth between his shoulders, so the Prophet ﷺ stayed in prostration. They laughed so hard that they were about to fall on each other. Someone went to Fatimah, with whom Allah is pleased, who was a young girl, and informed her of what had happened. She hurriedly came towards the Prophet ﷺ and removed the filth from his back, and then she turned around and she cursed the Quraishites who were sitting in that sitting. (Bukhari #498)

Muneeb al-Azdi said: 'I saw the Messenger of Allah in the Era of Ignorance saying to people:

'Say there is no god worthy of being worshipped except Allah if you would be successful.' There were those who spat in his face, and those who threw soil in his face, and those who swore at him until midday. Whenever a certain young girl came with a big container of water, and he would wash his face and hands and say: 'O daughter do not fear that your father will be humiliated or struck by poverty.' (Mu'jam al-Kabeer # 805)

Urwah b. az-Zubair said, 'I asked Abdullah b. Amr al-Aas to tell me of the worst thing the pagans did to the Prophet ﷺ and he said:

'Uqbah b. Mu'ait approached the Prophet ﷺ while he was praying near the Ka'bah, and he twisted his garment around his neck. Abu Bakr, with whom Allah is pleased, hurriedly approached and grabbed Uqbah's shoulder and pushed him away saying: 'Do you kill a man because he proclaims Allah as his *Rubb*, and clear signs have come to you from your *Rubb*?' (Bukhari 3643)

These incidents did not stop the Prophet ﷺ from giving Da'wah. He called the many tribes that came to Makkah for Hajj to Islam. A few believed from the people of Yathrib, which is known today as Madinah, and they pledged to support him and help him if he chose to go with them to Madinah. He sent with them Mus'ab b. Umair, with whom Allah is pleased, who taught them Islam. After all the hardships that the Muslims of Makkah faced from their own people, Allah allowed them to migrate from their city to Madinah. The people of Madinah greeted them and received them in a most extraordinary manner. Madinah became the Capital of the Islamic state, and the point from which the Da'wah was spread.

The Prophet ﷺ settled there and taught people Qur'anic recitation and Islamic Jurisprudence. The inhabitants of Madinah were greatly moved and touched by the Prophet's manners. They loved him more than they loved their own selves; they would rush to serve him, and spend all they had in his path. The society was strong and its people were rich in terms of *Iman* (Faith) and they were extremely happy. People loved each other, and true brotherhood was apparent amongst its people. All people were equal; the rich, noble and poor, black and white, Arab and non-Arab - they were all considered as equals in the *Deen* of Allah, no distinction was made among them except through piety. After the Quraish learnt of the

Prophet's Da'wah and that it had spread, they fought with the Prophet 🕮 in the first battle in Islam, the Battle of Badr. This battle took place between two groups which were unequal in preparations and weapons. The Muslims were 314; whereas, the pagans were 1000 strong. Allah gave victory to the Prophet 🕮 and the Companions. After this battle, many battles took place between the Muslims and the pagans. After eight years the Prophet 🕮 was able to prepare an army 10,000 strong. They headed towards Makkah and conquered it, and with this he defeated his people, who had harmed him and tortured his Companions in every way. They had even been forced to leave their property and wealth behind and flee for their lives. He decisively defeated them, and this year was called 'The Year of the Conquest.' Allah, the Exalted, says:

❨When the victory of Allah has come and the conquest, and you see the people entering into the *Deen* of Allah in multitudes, then exalt him with praise of your *Rubb* and ask forgiveness of Him. Indeed, He is ever accepting of repentance.❩ [110:1-3]

He then gathered the people of Makkah and said to them:

'What do you think I will do to you?' They answered: 'You will only do something favorable; you are a kind and generous brother, and a kind and generous nephew!' The Prophet 🕮 said: 'Go - you are free to do as you wish.'

(Baihaqi #18055)

This was one of the main reasons why many of them accepted Islam. The Prophet 🕮 then returned to Madinah. After a period of time, the Prophet 🕮 meant to perform Hajj, so he headed towards Makkah with 114,000 Companions and performed Hajj. This Hajj is known as *'Haj'jatul-Wa'daa'* or the 'Farewell

Pilgrimage' since the Prophet 📿 never performed another Hajj, and died shortly after he performed it.

The Prophet 📿 died in Madinah on the 12th day of Rabi ath-thani in the 11th year of Hijrah. The Prophet 📿 was buried in Madinah as well. The Muslims were shocked when they learnt of his death; some Companions did not believe it! Umar, with whom Allah is pleased, said: 'Whoever says that Muhammad is dead, I will behead him!' Abu Bakr, with whom Allah is pleased, then gave a speech, and read the words of Allah:

❨Muhammad is not but a Messenger. Other messengers have passed away before him. So if he was to die or be killed, would you turn back on your heels to unbelief? And He who turns back on his heels will never harm Allah at all; but Allah will reward the grateful.❩ [3:144]

When Umar, with whom Allah is pleased, heard this verse he stopped saying what he was saying, since he was very keen on applying the rules of Allah. The Prophet 📿 was 63 years old when he died.

He stayed in Makkah for forty years, before being commissioned as a prophet. After being commissioned as a Prophet; he lived there for another 13 years in which he called people to *Tawheed* (true monotheism). He then migrated to Madinah, and stayed there for ten years. He continuously received the revelation there, until the Qur'an and the *Deen* of Islam were complete.

George Bernard Shaw[3] said:

'I have always held the religion of Muhammad in high estimation because of its wonderful vitality. It is the only religion which appears to possess that assimilating capability to the changing phases of existence which make itself appeal to every age - I have prophesized about the faith of Muhammad that it would be acceptable tomorrow as it is beginning to be acceptable to the Europe of today. Medieval ecclesiastics, either through ignorance or bigotry, painted Muhammadanism in the darkest colours. They were, in fact, trained to hate both the man Muhammad and his religion. To them, Muhammad was an anti-Christ. I have studied him, the wonderful man, and in my opinion, far from being an anti-Christ, he must be called the Saviour of humanity - '[4]

---

[3] He was a famous writer and critic. He died in 1950.
[4] Encyclopedia of Seerah, by Afzalur Rahman.

The Description of the Prophet 🕮:

Hind the daughter of Abu Haalah at-Tamimi, with whom Allah is pleased, described the Prophet of Allah 🕮 with the following description:

The Messenger of Allah 🕮 was a sensational man, who was honored by all who saw him. His face glowed like the full moon. He was of moderate height, not too tall and not too short. He had a large head and his hair was wavy. He would part his hair if it got long, otherwise, his hair did not exceed the lobes of his ears under normal circumstances. He was a healthy pink. His forehead was wide. His eyebrows were naturally groomed, and were not joined. There was a vein between his eyebrows that swelled in case of anger. His nose was straight and had a special glow. The bridge of his nose was slightly high. He 🕮 had a thick beard with soft cheeks. His mouth was slightly large. He had moustaches. His teeth had gaps in between. His neck was [pretty] like that of a doll, and it was silvery white. He 🕮 was moderately built and very strong. His belly and chest were on the same level. His chest and shoulders were wide. His body joints were big. His skin was white. He had hair from the end of his breastbone to his navel. There was no hair on his breasts, but his arms and shoulders were hairy. His forearms were large and his palms were wide. Both his hands and feet were short, and his fingers were of moderate length. His feet were flat and smooth; due to the smoothness of his feet water would not settle on them. He walked in strides and in a graceful manner; he would lift his feet, and not drag them. Whenever he 🕮 turned he would turn with his entire body [as opposed to turning his neck and head only]. He lowered his gaze at all times. He looked down to earth more often than he looked up to the heaven. He often glimpsed at things [as opposed to staring at things]. He offered the greetings to others before they offered it to him.'

Someone asked: 'Describe his manner of speech.' Hind said: 'The Prophet 🕮 appeared sad most of the time, and would be in deep thought. He would never rest completely, and he did not speak unless he needed to. Whenever he spoke he would start and complete his statements with the name of Allah. He spoke clearly and uttered meaningful, precise and accurate statements only. His statements were very decisive; no one could distort his words. He was extremely kind and caring. He never insulted others. He was grateful for every blessing Allah bestowed on him, no matter how minute it seemed; he never belittled anything. He did not criticize any food he tasted, nor did he praise it. He was never upset for worldly affairs. If a person was wronged he would become very angry. His anger would not subside until the person's right was given to him. He would not become angry if he was wronged, nor would he avenge himself. When he pointed, he pointed with his entire hand; when he was surprised he would flip his hand. When the Prophet 🕮 talked he would tap his right palm using his left thumb. When he was angry he would turn his face away, and when he was pleased and happy he would lower his gaze. Most of his laughter was done by smiling. Whenever he smiled, his teeth appeared like pearls of hail.'

Al-Hasan 🕮 said: 'I did not inform al-Husain about this (description of the Prophet) for a period of time, but he had already asked his father (Ali 🕮) about these details. Al-

Husain 🕳 said: 'I asked my father about how the Prophet 🕌 entered upon his family, and left them and about his manners in general.' Al-Husain 🕳 said: 'I asked my father how the Prophet 🕌 spent his time in his house, and how he divided his time.' He replied: 'He divided his time into three portions; one portion for the sake of Allah, the other for his family, and the third he divided between himself and people. He did not conceal any advice or guidance from any of them. He would spend the portion he allotted for his Ummah by attending to the needs of people according to their religious status and needs. He would busy these people by teaching them that which would benefit them and their Ummah, and by informing them of what they needed. He would say to them: 'Let those who are present convey (what they have learned) to those who are absent, and inform me of the needs of those who cannot attend our sitting, for: 'Whoever informs the ruler of a person's plight, Allah would affirm him on the bridge on the Day of Resurrection.'

Al-Husain 🕳 further said, 'I asked my father about the manners of the Prophet 🕌 while he was outside his home?' He said, 'He safeguarded his tongue [from idle talk] and gave sincere counseling and talked with beneficial speech by which he would be able to gather and unite people. He honored the generous, kind and noble person amongst each people, and he would charge them with the affairs of their people. He warned people against evils and guarded himself against them as well, though he never frowned in the face of any person. He asked about people's situation and ordered with the good and forbade evil. He 🕌 was moderate in all his affairs. He never wasted an opportunity to remind his companions and give them sincere counseling. He 🕮 was prepared for every case, and would uphold the truth and was not heedless. The people who sat nearest to him were the best among people. The best Companion was him who offered the best advice. The Companion highest in rank was the one who supported and helped him in the best manner.

Al-Husain 🕮 said: 'I asked my father how the Prophet 🕮 behaved in his sittings, and he said, 'The Messenger of Allah 🕮 never got up or sat down without mentioning the name of Allah. He forbade designating a certain spot to a person so that he would consider it as his own. He sat wherever he found a spot. He also ordered others to do the same, when they entered a sitting. He divided his time equally and justly among his Companions who sat with him. The one who sat with the Prophet 🕮 would think that he was the most important and beloved individual to him. If a person came asking him for a certain need, he would not rush him, rather he would allow the person to complete his request and leave at his own accord. The Prophet 🕮 would not return one who asked empty-handed; he would even say nice words to him if he was not able to fulfill his request. He had an open heart and an open mind. He was considered like a kind and caring father to everyone; all people were to him equal. His sittings were sittings of knowledge, perseverance, patience, modesty, and trust. No one would raise his voice in the presence of the Messenger of Allah 🕮. No one talked evil about another in his presence either. Those in the sitting treated each other in a humble manner, and they respected the elderly and were merciful to the young and they respected the stranger.'

Al-Husain 鐭 said: 'I asked my father about the Prophet's attitude with people in his meetings and sittings, and he said to me: 'The Messenger of Allah 鐭 was constantly cheerful. He was extremely kind and caring. He was never rough. He never raised his voice in public or used foul language. He never talked ill of anyone or gossiped. He never adulated anyone. He never disappointed anyone. He avoided three things; argumentation, talking too much and interfering in what is of no importance to him. He also avoided three other things; he never talked ill of anyone, he never mocked anyone and he never spoke of anyone's fault in front of others, nor did he criticize anyone. He spoke only about things that he hoped to be rewarded for. Whenever he spoke his Companions looked at the ground [out of respect and attention] it was as if birds landed on their heads. When the Messenger of Allah 鐭 stopped talking, his Companions talked. They never differed in front of him. Whenever one of his Companions talked, the rest would attentively listen until he completed his statement. Only leading Companions talked in the presence of the Messenger of Allah 鐭.

The Messenger of Allah 鐭 demonstrated extreme patience when he listened to a stranger with a difficult accent or dialect. He would not ask the speaker any question until he completed his statement. In fact, the Messenger of Allah 鐭 directed his Companions to assist the person who sought his help. He never interrupted a speaker until the speaker completed his statement and stopped at his own accord or if the person got up to leave.' (Baihaqi)

Some of the Prophet's Manners & Characteristics:

1. **Sound Intellect:** The Messenger 靏 had an excellent, complete and sound intellect. No man has ever had an intellect as complete and perfect as his. Qadhi Iyaadh, may Allah have mercy on him, said:

> 'This becomes clear to an individual when the researcher reads the Prophet's biography and understands his state of affairs, and his meaningful and inclusive utterances and traditions, his good manners, ethics and moral character, his knowledge of the Torah and Gospel and other Divine Scriptures, and his knowledge of statements of the wise, and knowledge of bygone nations, and ability to strike examples and implement policies and correct emotional manners. He was an example and paradigm to which his people related to in all branches of knowledge; acts of worship, medicine, laws of inheritance, lineage, and other matters as well. He knew and learned all of this without reading or examining the Scriptures of those before us, nor did he sit with their scholars. The Prophet had no formal schooling, and was without knowledge of the above before being commissioned as a Prophet, nor could he read or write. The Prophet 靏 was wise to the fullest extent of his mental capacity. Allah, the Exalted, informed him of some of what had taken place (in the past) and of that which would take place in the future. This is a sign that the Dominion belongs to Allah, and that He is capable over all things.'[5]

---

[5] Qadhi Eiyadh, 'Al-Shifa bita'reefi Hoquooqil-Mostafa',

2. **Doing Things for the Sake of Allah**: The Prophet ﷺ would always do deeds through which he would seek the pleasure of Allah. He was harmed and abused when he invited and called people to Islam; yet he was patient and endured all of this, and hoped for the reward of Allah. Abdullah b. Masood, with whom Allah is pleased, said:

'It is as though I am looking at the Prophet ﷺ talking about a Prophet who was hurt by his people. He wiped the blood from his face and said: 'O Allah! Forgive my people, for they know not!' (Bukhari #3290)

Jundub b. Sufyaan, with whom Allah is pleased, said that the Messenger's finger bled during one of the battles, and he said:

'You are but a finger which has bled; which suffers in the path of Allah.' (Bukhari #2648)

3. **Sincerity**: The Prophet ﷺ was sincere and honest in all his matters, as Allah had ordered him. Allah, the Exalted, said:

❨Say, 'Indeed, my prayer, my rites of sacrifice, my living and my dying are for Allah, *Rubb* of the worlds. No partner has He. And this I have been commanded, and I am the first (among you) of the Muslims.❩ [6:162-163]

4. **Good Morals, Ethics and Companionship**: The narrator said,

"I asked A'ishah, with whom Allah is pleased, to inform me of the Prophet's manners, and she said: **'His manners were the Qur'an'"**

This means that the Prophet ﷺ abided by its laws and commands and abstained from its prohibitions. He would observe the virtuous deeds mentioned in it. The Prophet ﷺ said:

'Allah has sent me to perfect good manners and to do good deeds.' (Bukhari & Ahmed)

Allah, the Exalted, described the Prophet 🕮 saying:

《And indeed, you are of a great moral character》 [68:4]

Anas b. Malik, with whom Allah is pleased, who was the servant of the Prophet 🕮 for ten years; day in and day out, during the Prophet's travels and when he was a resident in Madinah. Throughout this period of time, he knew of the Prophet's manners. He said:

'The Prophet 🕮 did not swear at anyone, nor was he rude, nor did he curse anyone. When he blamed anyone he would say: 'What is wrong with him, may dust be cast in his face.' (Bukhari #5684)

5. **Politeness and Good Manners**: Sahl b. Sa'd, with whom Allah is pleased, reported:

"A drink was brought to the Prophet 🕮 and he drank from it. On his right side there was a young boy and on his left side were elderly men. He asked the young boy: 'Do you mind if I give the drink to them?' The young boy said: 'O Prophet of Allah! By Allah! I would not prefer anyone to drink from thFe place you drank. This is my fair share [due to sitting to your right].' The Messenger of Allah 🕮 handed the boy the drink." (Bukhari #2319)

6. **Love for Reformation and Reconciliation**: Sahl b. Sa'd, with whom Allah is pleased, said that the people of *Qubaa'* fought amongst themselves and threw rocks at each other. The Prophet 🕮 said:

'Let us go to resolve the situation and make peace between them.' (Bukhari #2547)

7. **Ordering with the good and forbidding evil**: Abdullah b. Abbas, with whom Allah is pleased, said:

The Messenger of Allah ﷺ saw a man wearing a gold ring, so he reached for it, removed it and threw it. He then said:

'Would one of you seek a burning charcoal and place it on his hand?!'

The man was later told, after the Prophet ﷺ left: 'Take your ring! Make good use of it [by selling it].' The man said: 'No, by Allah! I will never take it after the Messenger of Allah ﷺ threw it away.' (Muslim #2090)

8. **Love of Purification**: Muhaajir b. Qunfudth, with whom Allah is pleased, reported that he passed by the Prophet ﷺ while he was urinating; he greeted him with Salaam, but the Prophet ﷺ did not return the greeting until he made wudhu and apologized saying:

'I disliked that I should mention Allah's name while I am not in a state of purity.'   (Ibn Khuzaimah #206)

9. **Safeguarding and Minding One's Language**: Abdullah b. Abi O'faa, with whom Allah is pleased, said that the Messenger of Allah ﷺ would busy himself with the remembrance of Allah; he would not talk in vain. He would lengthen his prayers and shorten the speech, and he would not hesitate to help and take care of the needs of a needy, poor or widow.   (Ibn Hib'ban #6423)

10. **Excelling in Acts of Worship**: A'ishah, with whom Allah is pleased, said that the Prophet of Allah ﷺ used to pray during the night until his feet would swell.

A'ishah, said: 'Why do you do this, O Messenger of Allah, and Allah has forgiven your past and future sins?' The Prophet ﷺ said: **'Shall I not be a grateful slave?'**   (Bukhari #4557)

11. **Forbearance and Kindness**: Abu Hurairah, with whom Allah is pleased, said At-Tufail b. Amr ad-Dawsi and his companions came to meet the Prophet ﷺ.

They said: 'O Messenger of Allah, the tribe of *Daws*, has refused to accept Islam, so supplicate Allah against them. It was said: 'the tribe of *Daws* is doomed and destroyed!' The Prophet ﷺ raised his hands and said: '**O Allah guide the tribe of *Daws* and bring them!**'

12. **Good Appearance**: Al-Baraa' b. Aazib, with whom Allah is pleased, said:

'**The Prophet ﷺ was a person of average height. His shoulders were wide. His hair reached his earlobes. Once I saw him adorned in a red garment; I never saw anything more beautiful than him.**' (Bukhari #2358)

13. **Asceticism in Worldly Affairs**: Abdullah b. Masood, with whom Allah is pleased, said:

'**The Messenger of Allah ﷺ went to sleep on a mat. He got up and he had marks on his side due to the mat that he had slept on. We said: 'O Messenger of Allah, shall we not make bedding for you?' He said: 'What do I have to do with this world? I am only like a wayfarer who rides a beast that stopped to take shade and rest under a tree, and then leaves it behind and continues on the journey.**'

(Tirmidthi #2377)

Amr' b. al-Haarith, with whom Allah is pleased, said the Messenger of Allah ﷺ did not leave a *Dirham* or *Dinar*, or slave, male or female, after his death. He only left behind his white mule, his weapons and a piece of land which he declared as *Sadaqah* (charity).' (Bukhari #2588)

14. **Altruism:** Sahl b. Sa'd, with whom Allah is pleased, said:

'A woman gave the Messenger of Allah 🕌 a *Burdah* (gown). The Prophet 🕌 asked his Companions: 'Do you know what a *Burdah* is?' They replied, 'Yes, O Prophet of Allah! It is a piece of woven cloth [similar to a shawl]. The woman said: 'O Prophet of Allah! I have woven this shawl with my own hands, for you to wear.' The Messenger of Allah 🕌 took it while he direly needed it. After a while, the Messenger of Allah 🕌 came out of his home wearing it, and a Companion said to the Messenger of Allah 🕌: 'O Prophet of Allah! Grant me this shawl to wear!' The Messenger of Allah 🕌 said: 'Yes.' He thereafter sat for awhile, and headed back home, folded it and gave it to the person who asked for it. The Companions, with whom Allah is pleased, scolded him saying: 'It was not appropriate for you to ask for his shawl; especially since you know he would not turn anyone down, or send them away empty-handed! The man said: 'By Allah! I only asked him to give it to me because I want to be shrouded in this shawl when I die.' Sahl, the narrator of the Hadeeth, with whom Allah is pleased, said: 'The shawl was used as a shroud for that man when he died.' (Bukhari #1987)

15. **Strong Faith and Dependence on Allah:** Abu Bakr, with whom Allah is pleased, said:

'I looked at the feet of the pagans while we were in the cave [of *Thawr*]. I said, "O Prophet of Allah! If anyone of them looks down at his feet he would see us!' The Messenger of Allah 🕌 said: 'O Abu Bakr! What do you think of, two with whom Allah, the Exalted, is their Third?' (Muslim #1854)

16. **Kindness and Compassion**: Abu Qatadah, with whom Allah is pleased, said:

'The Messenger of Allah 鐵 performed *Salah* (prayer) while he was carrying a young girl named Umaamah, daughter of Abul-Aas. When he bowed, he put her on the ground, and when he stood up, he would carry her again.'

(Bukhari #5650)

17. **Simplification and Ease**: Anas, with whom Allah is pleased, said that the Messenger of Allah 鐵 said:

'I start the prayer with the intention of lengthening it, but when I hear a child crying, I shorten the prayer as I know the mother of that child would suffer from his screams!'

(Bukhari #677)

18. **Fearing Allah, being Mindful to not trespass His Limits and Devotion**: Abu Hurairah, with whom Allah is pleased, said that the Messenger of Allah 鐵 said:

'Sometimes, when I return to my family, I would find a date-fruit on the bed. I would pick it up to eat it; but I would fear that it was from the charity, and thus, throw it back [on the ground].' (Bukhari #2300)

19. **Expending Generously**: Anas bin Malik, with whom Allah is pleased, said:

'The Messenger of Allah 鐵 was never asked for something when someone accepted Islam, except that he granted that person what he asked. A man came to the Prophet 鐵 and he gave him a herd of sheep that was grazing between two mountains. The man returned to his people and said: 'O my people accept Islam! Muhammad

ﷺ gives out generously like one who does not fear poverty.' (Muslim #2312)

20. **Cooperation**: A'ishah, with whom Allah is pleased, was once asked about how the Prophet ﷺ behaved with his family. She said:

'He helped and assisted his family members with their chores; but when the call to prayer was heard, he would leave to attend the prayers.'

Al-Baraa bin 'Azib, with whom Allah is pleased, said:

'**I saw the Messenger of Allah ﷺ on the Day of the Trench carrying dirt [that was dug from the trench] until the dirt covered his chest. He was quite hairy. I heard him saying a few lines of Abdullah b. Rawaahah's poetry: 'O Allah! Had it not been for You, We would have never been guided, nor offered prayers or give in charity. O Allah! Let tranquility descend upon us, and make us firm when we meet our enemies. Verily they have transgressed against us! And if they wish for an affliction we reject and refuse it! He ﷺ raised his voice while saying these lines of poetry.'** (Bukhari #2780)

21. **Truthfulness**: A'ishah, with whom Allah is pleased, said:

'The trait and characteristic which the Prophet ﷺ hated most was lying. A man would tell a lie in the presence of the Prophet ﷺ and he would hold it against him, until he knew that he repented.' (Tirmidthi 1973)

Even his enemies attested to his truthfulness. Abu Jahl, who was one of the harshest enemies, said: 'O Muhammad! I do not say that you are a liar! I only deny what you brought and what you call people to.' Allah, the Exalted, says:

❨We know indeed that what they say certainly grieves you, but surely they do not call you a liar; but the unjust deny the verses of Allah.❩ [6:33]

22. **Aggrandizing the limits and boundaries of Allah**: A'ishah, with whom Allah is pleased, said:

'The Prophet ﷺ was not given a choice between two matters, except that he chose the easier of the two, as long as it was not a sinful act. If that act was a sinful act, he would be the farthest from it. By Allah! He never avenged himself. He only became angry when people transgressed the limits and boundaries of Allah; in that case he avenged.' (Bukhari #6404)

23. **Pleasant Facial Expression**: Abdullah bin al-Harith, with whom Allah is pleased, said:

'I have never seen a man who smiled as much as the Messenger of Allah ﷺ.' (Tirmidthi #2641)

24. **Honesty and Loyalty**: The Prophet ﷺ was well-known for his honesty. The pagans of Makkah -who were openly hostile towards him- would leave their valuables with him. His honesty and loyalty was tested when the pagans of Makkah abused him and tortured his companions and drove them out of their homes. He ordered his cousin, Ali b. Abi Talib, with whom Allah is pleased, to postpone his migration for three days to return to people their valuables.[6]

Another example of his honesty and loyalty is demonstrated in the Truce of *Hudaibiyah*, wherein he agreed to the article in the treaty which stated that any man who left the Prophet ﷺ would not be returned to him, and any man who left Makkah would

---

[6] Ibn Hisham's Biography, Vol. 1, p.493 [Arabic Edition].

be returned to them. Before the treaty was concluded a man named Abu Jandal b. Amr had managed to escape from the pagans of Makkah and rushed to join Muhammad ﷺ. The pagans asked Muhammad to honor his pledge and return the escapee. The Messenger of Allah ﷺ said:

'O Abu Jandal! Be patient and ask Allah to grant you patience. Allah will surely help you and those who are persecuted and make it easy for you. We have signed an agreement with them, and we certainly do not betray or act treacherously.' (Baihaquee #18611)

25. Bravery and courage: Ali, with whom Allah is pleased, said:

'You should have seen me on the Day of Badr! We sought refuge with the Messenger of Allah ﷺ. He was the closest among us to the enemy. On that Day, the Messenger of Allah ﷺ was the strongest one among us.' (Ahmed #654)

As for his courage and bravery under normal circumstances - Anas b. Malik, with whom Allah is pleased, said:

'The Messenger of Allah ﷺ was the best of people and the most courageous. One night, the people of Madinah were frightened and headed towards the sounds they heard during the night. The Messenger of Allah ﷺ met them while coming back from the place of the sound, after he made sure that there was no trouble. He was riding a horse that belonged to Abu Talhah, with whom Allah is pleased, without any saddle, and he had his sword with him. He was assuring the people, saying: 'Do not be frightened! Do not be frightened!' (Bukhari #2751)

He met up with people riding a horse with no saddle, and he carried his sword, for there might be a reason or need to use it.

He did not wait for others to check out the source of trouble; as is done in these situations.

In the Battle of Uhud, the Messenger of Allah 🕌 consulted his Companions. They advised him to fight, while he himself did not see the need to fight. However, he took their advice. The Companions, upon learning the Prophet's feelings regretted what they had done. The Ansaris said to him, 'O Prophet of Allah! Do as you please.' But, he replied:

'It does not befit a Prophet who has worn his war attire to remove it until he fights.' (Ahmed #14829)

26. Generosity and Hospitality: Ibn Ab'bas, with whom Allah is pleased, said:

'The Prophet 🕌 was the most generous of people. He was most generous during Ramadhan when he met Jibreel 🕌; he would meet him every night during Ramadhan to practice and review the Qur'an with him. The Messenger of Allah 🕌 was so generous, that he was faster than the swiftest wind in this regard. (Bukhari #6)

Abu Dharr, with whom Allah is pleased, said:

'I was walking with the Prophet 🕌 in the *Har'rah* (volcanic region) of Madinah and we faced the mount of Uhud; the Prophet 🕌 said: 'O Abu Dharr!' I said: 'Here I am O Messenger of Allah!' He said: 'It would not please me to have an amount of gold equal to the weight of Mount Uhud, until I expend and give out (in the sake of Allah) within a night or within three nights. I would keep a Dinar of it to help those who are in debt. (Bukhari #2312)

Jabir b. Abdullah, with whom Allah is pleased, said:

'The Prophet 🕮 did not refuse to give anything which he had, to someone if he asked for it.' (Bukhari #5687)

27. **Bashfulness and Modesty**: Abu Sa'eed al-Khudri, with whom Allah is pleased, said:

'The Prophet 🕮 was more modest and bashful than a virgin who hides in the women's quarter of the tent. If he hated or disliked something, we could sense it from his facial expressions.' (Bukhari #5751)

28. **Humbleness**: The Messenger of Allah 🕮 was the most humble person. He was so humble that if a stranger were to enter the Masjid and approach the Prophet's sitting place and he was sitting with his Companions one would not be able to distinguish him from his Companions.

Anas bin Malik, with whom Allah is pleased, said:

'Once, while we were sitting with the Messenger of Allah 🕮 in the Masjid, a man on his camel came in, after he tied it with a rope, he asked: 'Who of you is Muhammad?' The Messenger of Allah 🕮 was sitting on the ground while he was leaning, with his Companions. We directed the Bedouin, saying: 'This white man, who is leaning on the ground.' The Prophet 🕮 did not differ nor distinguish himself from his Companions.

The Prophet 🕮 would not hesitate to help the poor, needy and widows in their needs. Anas b. Malik, with whom Allah is pleased, said:

'A woman from the people of Madinah who was partially insane said to the Prophet 🕮: 'I have to ask you about something.' He helped her and took care of her needs.'

(Bukhari #670)

29. Mercy and Compassion: Abu Masood al-Ansari, with whom Allah is pleased, said:

'A man came to the Prophet 靉 and said: "O Messenger of Allah! By Allah! I do not pray Fajr prayer because so and so lengthens the prayer." He said: 'I have never seen the Messenger of Allah 靉 deliver a speech in such an angry state. He said:

'O People! Verily there are among you those who chase people away! If you lead people in prayer, shorten the prayer. There are old and weak people and those with special needs behind you in prayer.' (Bukhari #670)

Osama bin Zaid, with whom Allah is pleased, said:

'We were sitting with the Messenger of Allah 靉. One of his daughters sent a person calling him to visit her and see her son, who was on his deathbed. The Messenger of Allah 靉 told the person to tell her: 'Truly to Allah belongs what He took, and He has given everything a set time. Command her to be patient and to seek the reward of Allah, the Exalted.' His daughter, with whom Allah is pleased, sent the same person back again saying: 'O Prophet of Allah! Your daughter took an oath that you should come.' The Messenger of Allah 靉 got up, and Sa'd bin Ubaadah and Mu'adth bin Jabal accompanied him. The Messenger of Allah 靉 sat with the child while he was on his deathbed. The child's eyes froze in their places like stones. Upon seeing that, the Messenger of Allah 靉 wept. Sa'd said to him, 'What is this 'O Prophet of Allah?' He said: 'This is a mercy that Allah, the Exalted, places in the hearts of His slaves. Truly, Allah is merciful to those who are merciful towards others.' (Bukhari #6942)

30. **Perseverance and Forgiveness:** Anas bin Malik, with whom Allah is pleased, said:

'Once, I was walking with the Messenger of Allah 🌸 while he was wearing a Yemeni cloak with a collar with rough edges. A Bedouin grabbed him strongly. I looked at the side of his neck and saw that the edge of the cloak left a mark on his neck. The Bedouin said, 'O Muhammad! Give me [some] of the wealth of Allah that you have.' The Messenger of Allah 🌸 turned to the Bedouin, laughed and ordered that he be given [some money].' (Bukhari #2980)

Another example of his perseverance is the story of the Jewish Rabbi, Zaid bin Sa'nah. Zaid loaned the Messenger of Allah 🌸 something. Zaid said:

'Two or three days prior to the return of the debt, the Messenger of Allah 🌸 was attending the funeral of a man from the Ansar. Abu Bakr and Umar, Uthman and some other Companions, with whom Allah is pleased, were with the Prophet 🌸. After he prayed the *Jinazah* (funeral prayer) he sat down close to a wall, and I came towards him, grabbed him by the edges of his cloak and looked at him in a harsh way, and said: 'O Muhammad! Will you not pay me back my loan? I have not known the family of Abdul-Mutalib to delay in repaying debts!

I looked at Umar b. al-Khat'taab, with whom Allah is pleased - his eyes were swollen with anger! He looked at me and said: 'O Enemy of Allah, do you talk to the Messenger of Allah and behave towards him in this manner?! By the One who sent him with the truth, had it not been for the fear of missing it (Jannah) I would have beheaded you with my sword! The Prophet 🌸 was looking at Umar in a calm and peaceful manner, and he said: 'O Umar, you should have given us sincere counseling, rather than to do what you did! O Umar, go and repay him his loan, and give him twenty *Sa'a* (measurement of weight) extra because you scared him!'

Zaid said: 'Umar went with me, and repaid me the debt, and gave me over it twenty *Sa'a* of dates. I asked him: 'What is this?' He said: 'The Messenger of Allah ﷺ ordered me to give it, because I frightened you.' Zaid then asked Umar: 'O Umar, do you know who I am?' Umar said: 'No, I don't - who are you?' Zaid said: 'I am Zaid b. Sa'nah.' Umar inquired: 'The Rabbi?' Zaid answered: 'Yes, the Rabbi.' Umar then asked him: 'What made you say what you said to the Prophet ﷺ and do what you did to him?' Zaid answered: 'O Umar, I have seen all the signs of prophethood in the face of the Messenger of Allah ﷺ except two – (the first) his patience and perseverance precede his anger and the second, the more harsher you are towards him, the kinder and more patient he becomes, and I am now satisfied. O Umar, I hold you as a witness that I testify and am satisfied that there is no true god worthy of being worshipped except Allah alone, and my *Deen* is Islam and Muhammad ﷺ is my Prophet. I also hold you as a witness that half of my wealth - and I am among the wealthiest people in Madinah - I give for the sake of Allah to the entire Ummah.' Umar, with whom Allah is pleased, said: 'you will not be able to distribute your wealth to the whole Ummah (nation), so say, 'I will distribute it to some of the Ummah of Muhammad ﷺ.' Zaid said: 'I said, then I will distribute (the apportioned) wealth to some of the Ummah.' Both Zaid and Umar, with whom Allah is pleased, returned to the Messenger of Allah 🌸. Zaid said to him: 'I bear witness that there is no true god worthy of being worshipped except Allah alone, and that Muhammad 🌸 is the slave of Allah and His Messenger.' He believed in him, and witnessed many battles and then died in the Battle of Tabuk while he was encountering the enemy - may Allah have mercy on Zaid.'

(Ibn Hibban #288)

A great example of his forgiveness and perseverance is apparent when he pardoned the people of Makkah after its conquest. When the Messenger of Allah 🌸 gathered the people; who had abused, harmed and tortured him and his companions, and had driven them out of the city of Makkah, he said:

'What do you think I will do to you?' They answered: 'You will only do something favorable; you are a kind and generous brother, and a kind and generous nephew!' The Prophet 🌸 said: 'Go - you are free to do as you wish.'

(Baihaqi #18055)

31. **Patience:** The Messenger of Allah 🌸 was a paradigm of patience. He was patient with his people before calling them to Islam; for they would worship idols and do sinful acts. He was patient and tolerant with the abuse and harm the pagans of Makkah inflicted on him and his Companions and sought the reward of Allah. He also was patient and tolerant with the abuse of the hypocrites in Madinah.

He was a paradigm of patience when he lost his loved ones; his wife Khadeejah, died during his life. All his children died during his life, except for Fatimah, with whom Allah is pleased. His uncle Hamzah, with whom Allah is pleased, and Abu Talib passed away as well. The Prophet 🕮 was patient and sought the reward of Allah.

Anas b. Malik, with whom Allah is pleased, said:

> 'We entered the house of Abu Saif - the blacksmith - with the Prophet 🕮. Abu Saif's wife was the wet-nurse of his son, Ibraheem. The Messenger of Allah 🕮 lifted his son Ibraheem, and smelled and kissed him. After a while he went and saw his son again - he was dying. The Prophet 🕮 started to cry. Abdurrahmaan b. Auf, with whom Allah is pleased, said: 'O Prophet of Allah, you too cry!' The Messenger 🕮 said: 'O Ibn Auf, this is a mercy' - the Prophet 🕮 shed more tears and said: 'The eyes shed tears, the heart is saddened, and we only say what pleases our *Rubb*, and we are saddened by your death, O Ibraheem!'

(Bukhari #1241)

32. **Justice and Fairness**: The Messenger of Allah 🕮 was just and fair in every aspect of his life, and in the application of Shari'ah (Islamic Jurisprudential Law).

A'ishah, the mother of Believers, with whom Allah is pleased, said:

> 'The people of Quraish were extremely concerned about the Makhzoomi woman (i.e. the woman from the tribe of Bani Makhzoom) who committed a theft. They conversed among themselves and said, 'Who can intercede on her behalf with the Messenger of Allah 🕮?'

> They finally said: 'Who dares to speak to the Messenger of Allah 🕮 in this matter except Usamah b. Zaid, the most beloved young man to the Messenger of Allah 🕮.' So Usamah, with whom Allah is pleased, spoke to the

Messenger of Allah 🌸 regarding the woman. The Messenger of Allah 🌸 said:

'O Usamah! Do you intercede (on their behalf to disregard) one of Allah's castigations and punishments!'

The Messenger of Allah 🌸 got up and delivered a speech, saying:

'People before you were destroyed because when the noble among them stole, they would let him go; and if the poor and weak stole they would punish him. By Allah! If Fatimah, the daughter of Muhammad stole, I would cut her hand off.' (Bukhari #3288)

The Messenger of Allah 🌸 was just and fair and allowed others to avenge themselves if he harmed them. Usaid b. Hudhair, with whom Allah is pleased, said:

'A man from the Ansar, was cracking jokes with people and making them laugh, and the Prophet 🌸 passed by him, and poked him at his side lightly with a branch of a tree that he was carrying. The man exclaimed: 'O Prophet of Allah! Allow me to avenge myself!' The Prophet 🌸 said: 'Go Ahead!' The man said: 'O Messenger of Allah, you are wearing a garment, and I was not, when you poked me!' The Messenger of Allah 🌸 lifted his upper garment, and the Ansari kissed his body saying: 'I only meant to do this, O Messenger of Allah!' (Abu Dawood #5224)

33. Fearing Allah, and Being Mindful of Him: The Messenger of Allah 🌸 was the most mindful person of Allah. Abdullah bin Masoud, with whom Allah is pleased, said:

'[Once] the Messenger of Allah 🌸 said to me: 'Recite to me from the Qur'an!' Abdullah b. Masood, with whom Allah is pleased, said: 'Shall I recite it to you, and it is revealed to you!' The Prophet 🕮 said: 'Yes.' He said: 'I started to recite Surat an-Nisaa, until I reached the verse: ❨How then if We brought from each nation a witness, and We brought you as a witness against these people!❩ (4:41)

Upon hearing this verse, the Messenger of Allah 🕮 said: 'That is enough!' Abdullah b. Masood, with whom Allah is pleased, said, I turned around and saw the Messenger of Allah 🕮 crying.'   (Bukhari #4763)

A'ishah, the Mother of the Believers, with whom Allah is pleased, said:

'If the Messenger of Allah 🕮 saw dark clouds in the sky; he would pace forwards and backwards and would exit his house and enter it. As soon as it rained, the Prophet 🕮 would relax. A'ishah, with whom Allah is pleased, asked him about it, and he said: 'I do not know, it may be as some people said:

❨Then, when they saw the (penalty in the shape of) a cloud traversing the sky, coming to meet their valleys, they said: 'This cloud will give us rain! Nay, it is the (calamity) you were asking to be hastened! A wind wherein is a Grievous Penalty!❩[7] (46:24)

34. Satisfaction and Richness of the Heart: Umar b. al-Khattab, with whom Allah is pleased, said:

'I entered the Messenger's house and I found him sitting on a mat. He had a leather pillow stuffed with fibers. He had a pot of water by his feet, and there was some clothes hung on the wall. His side had marks due to the mat that he lay on. Umar, with whom Allah is pleased, wept when

---

[7] Bukhari #3034.

he saw this, and the Messenger 靈 asked him: 'Why do you weep?' Umar said: 'O Prophet of Allah! Khosrau and Caesar enjoy the best of this world, and you are suffering in poverty?!' He said: 'Aren't you pleased that they enjoy this world, and we will enjoy the Hereafter?' (Bukhari #4629)

35. **Hoping for Goodness Even for his Enemies:** A'ishah, the mother of the Believers, with whom Allah is pleased, said:

'I asked the Messenger of Allah 靈: "Did you face a day harder and more intense than the Battle of Uhud?" He replied: 'I suffered a lot from your people! The worst I suffered was on the Day of al-'Aqabah when I spoke to Ali b. Abd Yaleel b. Abd Kilaal (in order to support me) but he disappointed me and left me. I left the area while I was quite worried, and walked - when I reached an area called Qarn ath-Tha'alib, I raised my head to the sky and noticed a cloud that shaded me. Jibreel 靈 called me and said: 'O Muhammad! Allah, the Exalted, has heard what your people have said to you - and has sent the Angel in charge of the mountains, so you can command him to do what you please.' The Prophet 靈 said: 'The Angel in charge of the mountains called me saying: 'May Allah exalt your mention and render you safe from every derogatory thing! O Muhammad, I will do whatever you command me to do. If you like I can bring the *Akhshabain* mountains together and crush them all.' The Messenger of Allah 靈 said: 'It may be that Allah raises from among them a progeny who worship Allah alone and associate no partners with Him.' (Bukhari #3059)

Abdullah b. Umar, with whom Allah is pleased, said:

'When Abdullah b. Ubai b. Salool died, his son Abdullah b. Abdullah came to the Prophet 🌸 and asked him for his garment, so that they could shroud their father with it. He then asked the Prophet 🌸 to pray the *Jinazah* (funeral prayer) on him, and he got up to do so, but Umar, with whom Allah is pleased, grabbed the outer garment of the Prophet 🌸 and said: 'O Messenger of Allah! Will you pray on him, and Allah has forbidden you to do so! The Messenger of Allah 🌸 said: '**Allah has given me the choice, for He says:**

❨**Ask forgiveness for them or do not ask forgiveness for them; even if you ask forgiveness for them seventy times, Allah will not forgive them; this is because they disbelieve in Allah and His Messenger, and Allah does not guide the transgressing people.**❩ [9:80]

And I will ask for forgiveness for him more than seventy times.' Umar, with whom Allah is pleased, then said: 'He is a hypocrite!' The Prophet, performed the prayer, and Allah revealed:

❨**And never offer prayer for any one of them who dies and do not stand by his grave; surely they disbelieve in Allah and His Messenger, and they shall die in transgression.**❩ [9:84] (Bukhari #2400)

Some of the Prophet's Ethical Manners:

1. The Prophet's close relations with his Companions: This is well-known due to the fact that we have detailed reports about the Prophet's biography. The Prophet 🕊 is the example which we should emulate in all our matters. Jareer b. Abdullah, with whom Allah is pleased, said: 'The Prophet 🕊 did not prevent me from sitting with him, since I accepted Islam. He always smiled when he looked at me. I once complained to him, that I could not ride a horse and he hit me in my chest and supplicated Allah, saying:

>'O Allah! Steady him, and make him a person who guides others and a source of guidance.' (Bukhari #5739)

2. The Prophet 🕊 would entertain his Companions and joke with them: Anas b. Malik, with whom Allah is pleased, said the Messenger of Allah 🕊 was the most well mannered person. I had a young brother whose name was Abu Umair - he would play with a small bird called 'An-Nughair'. The Prophet 🕊 said to him:

'O Abu Umair, what did the Nughair do?!' while he was playing with it. (Muslim #2150)

The Prophet 🕊 did not only entertain and joke with his companions by word of mouth; rather, he sported and amused them as well. Anas b. Malik, with whom Allah is pleased, said:

'A Bedouin named Zahir b. Haram would give gifts to the Prophet 🕊 and he would prepare things for him as well. The Prophet 🕊 said: **'Zahir is our desert, and we are his city.'**

The Prophet 🕊 approached him while he was selling his goods, and the Prophet 🕊 hugged him from behind, and he could not see him. He then said: 'Let me go!' When he knew that it was the Prophet 🕊 who was hugging him, he pressed his back towards the Messenger's chest! The Messenger of Allah 🕊 then said: 'Who will buy this slave from me?' Zahir said: 'O Messenger of Allah, I am worthless!' The Messenger of Allah 🕊 said:

'You are not considered worthless by Allah!' or he said: 'You are valuable and precious to Allah.' (Ibn Hibban #5790)

3. **He would consult his Companions:** The Prophet 🕊 would consult his Companions, and take their opinions and points of view into consideration in issues and matters for which no textual proofs were revealed. Abu Hurairah, with whom Allah is pleased, said:

'I have not seen a person more keen for the sincere advice of his companions than the Messenger of Allah 🕊.' (Tirmidthi #1714)

4. **Visiting the sick, whether he was Muslim or non-Muslim:** The Prophet 🕊 was concerned about his Companions and would make sure that they were well. If he was told about a Companion who was sick, he would rush to visit him with the Companions that were present with him. He wouldn't only visit the Muslims who were sick; rather, he would visit even non-Muslims. Anas b. Malik, with whom Allah is pleased, said:

'A Jewish boy would serve the Prophet 🕊 and he fell sick, so the Prophet 🕊 said: 'Let us go and visit him.' They went to visit him, and found his father sitting by his head, and the Messenger of Allah 🕊 said: 'proclaim that there is no true god worthy of being worshipped except Allah alone' and I will intercede on your behalf on account of it on the Day of Resurrection.' The boy looked at his father, and the father said: 'Obey Abul-Qasim!' so the boy uttered: 'There is no true god worthy of being worshipped except Allah alone, and Muhammad 🕮 is the last Messenger.' The Messenger of Allah 🕮 said: 'All praise is due to Allah, Who saved him from the Fire of Hell.' (Ibn Hibban #2960)

5. He was grateful for people's goodness towards him, and would reward that generously: Abdullah b. Umar, with whom Allah is pleased, said that the Messenger of Allah 🕮 said:

'Whoever seeks refuge with Allah against your evil, then do not harm him. Whoever asks you by Allah, then give him. Whoever invites you, then accept his invitation. Whoever does a favor for you or an act of kindness, then repay him in a similar manner; but if you do not find that which you can reward him with, then supplicate Allah for him continuously, until you think you have repaid him.' (Ahmed #6106)

A'ishah, with whom Allah is pleased, said:

'The Messenger of Allah 🕮 would accept gifts, and reward generously on account of that.' (Bukhari #2445)

6. The Messenger's love for everything which is beautiful and good: Anas, with whom Allah is pleased, said:

'The hand of the Messenger of Allah 🕮 was softer than any silk that I had ever touched, and his scent was sweeter than any perfume that I had ever smelt.' (Bukhari #3368)

7. The Messenger of Allah 🕮 loved to help others by interceding on their behalf:

Abdullah b. Abbas, with whom Allah is pleased, said:

'The husband of Bareerah, with whom Allah is pleased, was a slave whose name was Mugheeth - I saw him walking behind her in the streets of Madinah crying, and his tears were falling off his beard. The Messenger of Allah 鑅 said to Al-Abbas: 'Doesn't it amaze you, how much Mugheeth loves Bareerah, and how much she hates Mugheeth!'

The Prophet 鑅 said to Bareerah: 'Why don't you go back to him?' She said to him: 'Are you commanding me to do so?' He said: 'No, but I am interceding on his behalf.' She said: 'I have no need for him.'   (Bukhari # 4875)

8. The Messenger of Allah 鑅 would serve himself: A'ishah, with whom Allah is pleased, said:

'I was asked how the Messenger of Allah 鑅 behaved in his house.' She said: 'He was like any man; he washed his clothes, milked his sheep, and served himself.'   (Ahmed 24998)

The Prophet's excellent manners, not only made him serve himself; rather, he would serve others as well. A'ishah, with whom Allah is pleased, said:

'I was asked how the Messenger of Allah 鑅 behaved in his house.' She said: 'He would help out in the house with the daily chores, and when he heard the Adthan he would leave for the Masjid.' (Bukhari 5048)

Statements of Justice and Equity:

1. **The German Poet, Wolfgang Goethe[8]**, said: 'I looked into history for a human paradigm and found it to be in Muhammad 🌸.'

2. **Professor Keith Moore[9]**, said in his book: "The Developing Human": It is clear to me that these statements must have come to Muhammad from God, or Allah, because most of this knowledge was not discovered until many centuries later. This proves to me that Muhammad must have been a messenger of God, or Allah.' He further said: 'I have no difficulty in my mind reconciling that this is a divine inspiration or revelation, which lead him to these statements.'

3. **Dr. Maurice Bucaille,** said in his book: "The Qur'an, and Modern Science": 'A totally objective examination of it [the Qur'an] in the light of modern knowledge, leads us to recognize the agreement between the two, as has been already noted on repeated occasions. It makes us deem it quite unthinkable for a man of Muhammad's time to have been the author of such statements, on account of the state of knowledge in his day. Such considerations are part of what gives the Qur'anic Revelation its unique place, and forces the impartial scientist to

---

[8] German writer and scientist. A master of poetry, drama, and the novel, he spent 50 years on his two-part dramatic poem *Faust* (published 1808 and 1832). He also conducted scientific research in various fields, notably botany, and held several governmental positions.

[9] He was the former President of the Canadian Association of Anatomists, Department of anatomy and cell biology, University of Toronto.

admit his inability to provide an explanation which calls solely upon materialistic reasoning.'

4. **Annie Besant**[10] in 'The Life and Teachings of Mohammad,' said: 'It is impossible for anyone who studies the life and character of the great Prophet of Arabia, who knew how he taught and how he lived, to feel anything but reverence for the mighty Prophet, one of the great messengers of the Supreme. And although in what I put to you I shall say many things which may be familiar to many, yet I myself feel, whenever I reread them, a new way of admiration, a new sense of reverence for that mighty Arabian teacher.'

5. **Dr. Gustav Weil** in 'History of the Islamic Peoples' said: 'Muhammad was a shining example to his people. His character was pure and stainless. His house, his dress, his food –they were characterized by a rare simplicity. So unpretentious was he that he would receive from his companions no special mark of reverence, nor would he accept any service from his slave which he could do for himself. He was accessible to all at all times. He visited the sick and was full of sympathy for all. Unlimited was his benevolence and generosity as also was his anxious care for the welfare of the community.'

6. **Maurice Gaudefroy** said: 'Muhammad was a prophet, not a theologian, a fact so evident that one is loath to state it. The men who surrounded him and constituted the influential elite of the primate Muslim community, contented themselves with

---

[10] English theosophist, philosopher, and political figure who advocated home rule and educational reforms in India.

obeying the law that he had proclaimed in the name of Allah and with following his teaching and example.'[11]

7. **Washington Irving**[12], said: 'His military triumphs awakened no pride nor vain glory as they would have done had they been effected by selfish purposes. In the time of his greatest power he maintained the same simplicity of manner and appearance as in the days of his adversity. So far from affecting regal state, he was displeased if, on entering a room, any unusual testimonial of respect was shown to him.'

8. **Marquis of Dufferin** said: 'It is to Mussulman science, to Mussulman art, and to Mussulman literature that Europe has been in a great measure indebted for its extrication from the darkness of the Middle Ages.'[13]

---

[11] Encyclopedia of Seerah, by Afzalur-Rahman
[12] He was a famous writer. He died in 1859.
[13] Encyclopedia of Seerah, by Afzalur-Rahman

The Wives of the Prophet ﷺ:

After the death of his first wife, Khadeejah, with whom Allah is pleased, the Prophet ﷺ married eleven women; all were divorcees, except for A'ishah, with whom Allah is pleased. Six of his wives were from the tribe of Quraish, and five were from different Arabian tribes, and one was from the Coptic Christians in Egypt.[14] She was the mother of Ibraheem.[15] The Prophet ﷺ said:

> 'If you own a Coptic Christian, treat them kindly for between us is a pledge and relationship.' (Abdurrazaaq #19325)

The Prophet ﷺ married these women for a number of reasons:

1. **Religious and legislative purpose**: The Prophet ﷺ married Zainab b. Jahsh, with whom Allah is pleased. The Arabs in the Era of Ignorance would prohibit a man from marrying the wife of his adopted son; they believed that the adopted son was like a man's actual son in all aspects. The Prophet ﷺ married her, although she was previously the wife of his adopted son, Zaid b. Harithah, with whom Allah is pleased. The Messenger of Allah ﷺ married her to abolish this belief. Allah, the Exalted, says:

---

[14] Her name was Maariyah al-Qibtiyah, with whom Allah is pleased. She was a slave-girl given to him by Al-Moqoqas, the ruler of Egypt. She accepted Islam and died during the Caliphate of Umar, with whom Allah is pleased.

[15] This is one of the many ways a slave is freed in Islam. If the slave-girl gives birth to a child, she is considered a 'mother of a child' and must be freed upon the death of her master.

❨And when you said to him to whom Allah had shown favor and to whom you had shown a favor: keep your wife to yourself and be careful of (your duty to) Allah; and you concealed in your soul what Allah would bring to light, and you feared men, and Allah had a greater right that you should fear Him. But when Zaid had accomplished his want of her, We gave have her to you as a wife, so that there should be no difficulty for the believers in respect of the wives of their adopted sons, when they have accomplished their want of them; and Allah's command shall be fulfilled..❩ (33:37)

2. **Political reasons and for the sake of** *Da'wah*, **and to invite people to Islam, and to gain the favor of the Arab tribes:** The Messenger of Allah 🕊️ married women from the largest and strongest Arab tribes. The Prophet 🕊️ ordered his Companions, with whom Allah is pleased, to do this as well. The Prophet 🕊️ said to Abdurrahmaan b. Auf, with whom Allah is pleased:

'If they obey you (i.e. accept Islam) then marry the daughter of the head of the tribe.'

Dr. Cahan said: 'Some of the aspects of his life may seem confusing to us due to present day mentality. The Messenger is criticized due to his obsession of attaining worldly desires and his nine wives, whom he married after the death of his wife Khadeejah, with whom Allah is pleased. It has been confirmed that most of these marriages were for political reasons, which were aimed to gain loyalty of some nobles, and tribes.'

3. **Social reasons:** The Prophet 🕊️ married some of his Companions' wives who had died, in Jihad or while giving

Da'wah. He married them even though they were older than him, and he did so to honor them and their husbands.

Veccia Vaglieri[16] in her book 'In Defense of Islam' said: 'Throughout the years of his youth, Muhammad 🕌 only married one woman, even though the sexuality of man is at its peak during this period. Although he lived in the society he lived in, wherein plural marriage was considered the general rule, and divorce was very easy - he only married one woman, although she was older than him. He was a faithful husband to her for twenty-five years, and did not marry another woman, except after her death. He at that time was fifty years old. He married each of his wives thereafter for a social, or political purpose; such that he wanted to honor the pious women, or wanted the loyalty of certain tribes so that Islam would spread amongst them. All the wives Muhammad 🕌 married were not virgin, nor were they young or beautiful; except for A'ishah, with whom Allah is pleased. So how can anyone claim that he was a lustful man? He was a man not a god. His wish to have a son may have also lead him to marry; for the children that he had from Khadeejah all died. Moreover, who undertook the financial responsibilities of his large family, without having large resources. He was just and fair towards them all and did not differentiate between them at all. He followed the practice of previous Prophets such as Musa, whom no one objected to their plural marriage. Is the reason why people object to the plural marriage of Muhammad 🕌 the fact that we know the minute details of his life, and know so little of the details of the lives of the Prophets before him?

---

[16] A famous Italian Orientalist.

Thomas Carlyle said: 'Mahomet himself, after all that can be said about him, was not a sensual man. We shall err widely if we consider this man as a common voluptuary, intent mainly on base enjoyments,--nay on enjoyments of any kind.'[17]

---

[17] 'Heroes, Hero-Worship and the Heroic in History'

Textual Proofs which support the Prophethood of Muhammad 🌸:

Proofs from the Qur'an:

1. Allah, the Exalted, says:

❮Muhammad is not the father of any of your men, but (he is) the Messenger of Allah, and the last of the Prophets: and Allah has full knowledge of all things.❯ (33:40)

2. Eesa 🌸 gave the glad tidings of Prophet Muhammad in the Gospel. Allah, the Exalted, says:

❮And remember, Jesus, the son of Mary, said: "O Children of Israel! I am the Messenger of Allah (sent) to you, confirming the Law (which came) before me, and giving Glad Tidings of a Messenger to come after me, whose name shall be Ahmad." But when he came to them with Clear Signs they said, 'This is evident sorcery!'❯ (61:6)

Proofs from the Sunnah:

The Prophet 🌸 said:

'My example and the example of the Prophets before me is like a man who built a house, which he built and perfected except for the space of one block; people would go round the house and stare in awe at its perfection and say, 'had it not been for this space!' The Prophet 🌸 said: 'I am that brick, I am the last of Prophets.' (Bukhari #3342)

Previous Scriptures:

Ataa' b. Yasaar, with whom Allah is pleased, said: 'I met Abdullah b. Amr b. al-Aas, with whom Allah is pleased, and I asked him:

'Tell me about the description of the Messenger of Allah 🕮 in the Torah.' He said: 'He is described in the Torah with some of what he is described in the Qur'an; 'We have indeed sent you as a witness (over mankind) and one who gives glad-tidings, and warns others, and one who protects and safeguards the commoners. You are My slave and Messenger; I called you *Mutawakkil* (The Trusted One). You are neither ill-mannered nor rude, nor do you raise your voice. You do not pay evil with evil; rather, you forgive and pardon. I will not collect his soul until I guide the nations, and until they say, 'There is no true god worthy of being worshipped except Allah alone' and until they clearly see the Truth.'

Ata, with whom Allah is pleased, said: I met Ka'b, the Rabbi, and asked him about this narration, and he did not differ with Abdullah b. Amr b. Al-Aas, with whom Allah is pleased, except for a minor difference in the wording of the narration.' (Baihaqi #13079)

Abdul-Ahad Dawud, said: 'but I have tried to base my arguments on portions of the Bible which hardly allow of any linguistic dispute. I would not go to Latin, Greek, or Aramaic, for that would be useless: I just give the following quotation in the very words of the Revised Version as published by the British and Foreign Bible Society.

We read the following words in the Book of Deuteronomy chapter xviii. verse 18: "I will raise them up a prophet from among their brethren, like unto thee; and I will put my words in his mouth." If these words do not apply to Prophet Muhammad, they still remain unfulfilled. Prophet Jesus himself never claimed to be the Prophet alluded to. Even his disciples were of the same opinion: they looked to the second coming of Jesus for the fulfillment of the prophecy. So far it is undisputed that the first coming of Jesus was not the advent of the "prophet like unto thee," and his second advent can hardly fulfill the words. Jesus, as is believed by his Church, will appear as a Judge and not as a law-giver; but the promised one has to come with a "fiery law" in "his right hand."

In ascertaining the personality of the promised prophet the other prophecy of Moses is, however, very helpful where it speaks of the shining forth of God from Paran, the mountain of Mecca. The words in the Book of Deuteronomy, chapter xxxiii. verse 2, run as follows: "The Lord came from Sinai, and rose up from Seir unto them; he shined forth from mount Paran, and he came with ten thousands of saints; from his right hand went a fiery law for them."

In these words the Lord has been compared with the sun. He comes from Sinai, he rises from Seir, but he shines in his full glory from Paran, where he had to appear with ten thousands of saints with a fiery law in his right hand. None of the Israelites, including Jesus, had anything to do with Paran. Hagar, with her son Ishmael, wandered in the wilderness of Beersheba, who afterwards dwelt in the wilderness of Paran (Gen. xxi. 21). He married an Egyptian woman, and through his first-born, Kedar, gave descent to the Arabs who from that time till now are the dwellers of the wilderness of Paran. And if Prophet Muhammad admittedly on all hands traces his descent to Ishmael through Kedar and he appeared as a prophet in the wilderness of Paran and reentered Mecca with ten thousand saints and gave a fiery law to his people, is not the prophecy above-mentioned fulfilled to its very letter?

The words of the prophecy in Habakkuk are especially noteworthy. His (the Holy One from Paran) glory covered the heavens and the earth was full of his praise. The word "praise" is very significant, as the very name Muhammad literally means "the praised one." Besides the Arabs, the inhabitants of the wilderness of Paran had also been promised a Revelation: "Let the wilderness and the cities thereof lift up their voice, the villages that Kedar doth inhabit: let the inhabitants of the rock sing, let them shout from the top of the mountains. Let them give glory unto the Lord, and declare His praise in the islands. The Lord shall go forth as a mighty man, he shall stir up jealousy like a man of war, he shall cry, yea, roar; he shall prevail against his enemies" (Isaiah).

In connection with it there are two other prophecies worthy of note where references have been made to Kedar. The one runs thus in chapter 1x. of Isaiah: "Arise, shine for thy light is come, and the glory of the Lord is risen upon thee ... The multitude of camels shall cover thee, the dromedaries of Midian and Ephah; all they from Sheba shall come.. All the flocks of Kedar shall be gathered together unto thee, the rams of Nebaioth shall minister unto thee: they shall come up with acceptance on mine altar, and I will glorify the house of my glory" (1-7). The other prophecy is again in Isaiah "The burden upon Arabia. In the forest in Arabia shall ye lodge, O ye travelling companies of Dedanim. The inhabitants of the land of Tema brought water to him that was thirsty, they prevented with their bread him that fled. For they fled from the swords and from the bent bow, and from the grievousness of war. For thus hath the Lord said unto me, Within a year, according to the years of an hireling, and all the glory of Kedar shall fail: And the residue of the number of archers, the mighty of the children of Kedar, shall be diminished" Read these prophecies in Isaiah in the light of one in Deuteronomy which speaks of the shining forth of God from Paran.

If Ishmael inhabited the wilderness of Paran, where he gave birth to Kedar, who is the ancestor of the Arabs; and if the sons of Kedar had to receive revelation from God; if the flocks of Kedar had to come up with acceptance to a Divine altar to glorify "the house of my glory" where the darkness had to cover the earth for some centuries, and then that very land had to receive light from God; and if all the glory of Kedar had to fail and the number of archers, the mighty men of the children of Kedar, had to diminish within a year after the one fled from the swords and from the bent bows - the Holy One from Paran (Habakkuk iii 3) is no one else than Prophet Muhammad. Prophet Muhammad is the holy offspring of Ishmael through Kedar, who settled in the wilderness of Paran. Muhammad is the only Prophet through whom the Arabs received revelation at the time when the darkness had covered the earth.

Through him God shone from Paran, and Mecca is the only place where the House of God is glorified and the flocks of Kedar come with acceptance on its altar. Prophet Muhammad was persecuted by his people and had to leave Mecca. He was thirsty and fled from the drawn sword and the bent bow, and within a year after his flight the descendants of Kedar meet him at Badr, the place of the first battle between the Meccans and the Prophet, the children of Kedar and their number of archers diminish and all the glory of Kedar fails. If the Holy Prophet is not to be accepted as the fulfillment of all these prophecies they will still remain unfulfilled. "The house of my glory" referred to in Isaiah IX is the house of God in Mecca and not the Church of Christ as thought by Christian commentators. The flocks of Kedar, as mentioned in verse 7, have never come to the Church of Christ; and it is a fact that the villages of Kedar and their inhabitants are the only people in the whole world who have remained impenetrable to any influence of the Church of Christ.

Again, the mention of 10,000 saints in Deuteronomy xxx 3 is very significant. He (God) shined forth from Paran, and he came with 10,000 of saints. Read the whole history of the wilderness of Paran and you will find no other event but when Mecca was conquered by the Prophet. He comes with 10,000 followers from Medina and re-enters "the house of my glory." He gives the fiery law to the world, which reduced to ashes all other laws. The Comforter - the Spirit of Truth - spoken of by Prophet Jesus was no other than Prophet Muhammad himself. It cannot be taken as the Holy Ghost, as the Church theology says. "It is expedient for you that I go away," says Jesus, "for if I go not away the Comforter will not come unto you, but if I depart I will send him unto you."

The words clearly show that the Comforter had to come after the departure of Jesus, and was not with him when he uttered these words. Are we to presume that Jesus was devoid of the Holy Ghost if his coming was conditional on the going of Jesus: besides, the way in which Jesus describes him makes him a human being, not a ghost. "He shall not speak of himself, but whatsoever he shall hear that he shall speak." Should we presume that the Holy Ghost and God are two distinct entities and that the Holy Ghost speaks of himself and also what he hears from God? The words of Jesus clearly refer to some messenger from God. He calls him the Spirit of Truth, and so the Koran speaks of Prophet Muhammad, **"No, indeed, he has brought the truth, and confirmed the Messengers." Ch.37:37** [18]

From the Gospel:

Jesus said: 'God shall take me up from the earth, and shall change the appearance of the traitor so that every one shall believe him to be me; nevertheless when he dieth an evil death, I shall abide in that dishonor for a long time in the world. But when Mohammed shall come, the sacred messenger of God, that infamy shall be taken away.' (*The Gospel of Barnabas*, Chapter 112)

He further said: 'Adam, having sprung up upon his feet saw in the air a writing that shone like the sun, which said: 'There is only one God, and Mohammed is the messenger of God.' Then with fatherly affection the first man kissed those words, and rubbed his eyes and said: "Blessed be that day when thou shalt come to the world." (*The Gospel of Barnabas*, Chapter 39)

---

[18] Muhammad in the Bible, Abdul-Ahad Dawud.

Intellectual proofs which support the Prophethood of the Messenger of Allah

1. The Prophet ﷺ was unlettered. He did not know how to read or write. He lived among a people who were unlettered as well. Therefore one cannot claim that the Qur'an was authored by Muhammad ﷺ! Allah, the Exalted, says:

❨And you did not recite any Book before it, nor did you write one with your right hand; in that case the liars would have doubted.❩ (29:48)

2. The Arabs were challenged to bring forth something similar to the Qur'an, and they were unable to do so! The beauty, structure and deep meanings of the Qur'an amazed the Arabs. The Qur'an is the everlasting miracle of Muhammad ﷺ. The Messenger of Allah ﷺ said:

'The miracles of the Prophets (before Muhammad ﷺ) were confined to their times. The miracle I have been given is the Qur'an, which is everlasting; therefore, I hope to have the most followers.' (Bukhari 4598)

Even though his people were eloquent and well known for their awesome poetry, Allah challenged them to produce similar to the Qur'an, but they couldn't. Allah then challenged them to produce a chapter similar to it, and they couldn't.

Allah says:

❨And if you are in doubt as to what We have sent down to Our slave, then produce a chapter like it, and call upon your helpers beside Allah, if you are truthful.❩ (2:23)

Allah challenges mankind at large to bring forth similar to the Qur'an. Allah says:

❨Say, 'if mankind and the Jinn gathered together to produce the like of this Qur'an, they could not produce the like thereof, even though they should help one another.❩ (17:88)

3. The Prophet 🕮 continued preaching and calling people to Islam, even though he faced many hardships and was confronted by his people, who were plotting to kill him. Yet the Prophet 🕮 continued preaching, and was patient. If he was an imposter - he would stop preaching and would have feared for his life.

W. Montgomery Watt said: 'His readiness to undergo persecution for his beliefs, the high moral character of the men who believed in him and looked up to him as a leader, and the greatness of his ultimate achievement - all argue his fundamental integrity. To suppose Muhammad an impostor raises more problems that it solves. Moreover, none of the great figures of history is so poorly appreciated in the West as Muhammad.... Thus, not merely must we credit Muhammad with essential honesty and integrity of purpose, if we are to understand him at all; if we are to correct the errors we have inherited from the past, we must not forget the conclusive proof is a much stricter requirement than a show of plausibility, and in a matter such as this only to be attained with difficulty.'

4. Every person loves the ornaments and beauties of this life, and would be swayed by these things. Allah, the Exalted, says:

❨Beautified for men is the love of desired things –women and children, and stored-up heaps of gold and silver, and pastured horses and cattle and crops. That is the provision of the present life; but it is Allah with Whom is an excellent abode.❩ (3:14)

Man, by his nature, is keen in acquiring ornaments and beauties of this world. People differ in the method they use to acquire these things. Some would resort to using lawful means to gain these things, while others would resort to using unlawful means to acquire these things.

If this is known (you should know that) Quraish tried to persuade the Prophet ﷺ to stop calling people to Islam. They told him that they would make him the master of Quraish, and marry him to the most beautiful women, and make him the most affluent man amongst them. He responded to these tempting offers, saying:

> 'By Allah, if they place the sun in my right hand, and the moon in my left hand to leave this matter, I would not leave it, until Allah makes it apparent, or I am killed calling people to it.' (Ibn Hisham)

Were the Prophet ﷺ an impostor he would have accepted this offer without hesitation.

Thomas Carlyle, said: 'They called him a prophet, you say? Why, he stood there face to face with them, here, not enshrined in any mystery, visibly clouting his own cloak, cobbling his own shoes, fighting, counseling ordering in the midst of them. They must have seen what kind of a man he was, let him be called what ye like. No emperor with his tiaras was obeyed as this man in a cloak of his own clouting. During three and twenty ears of rough, actual trial, I find something of a veritable hero necessary for that of itself.'[19]

5. It is well known that subjects and wealth of a kingdom are subjected to the will of the king, and his service. As for

---

[19] 'Heroes, Hero-Worship and the Heroic in History'

Muhammad he knew that this life was a transitory stage. Ibraheem b. Alqamah, with whom Allah is pleased, said that Abdullah said: 'The Prophet lay down on a straw mat which had marked his side, so I said: 'O Messenger of Allah! I ransom you with my mother and father! Allow us to put bedding on this mat that you lay on, so your side would not be affected and marked.' The Prophet said:

'My example in this life is like a rider who took rest under the shade of a tree then continued on his journey.' (Ibn Majah #4109)

An-Nu'man b. Basheer, with whom Allah is pleased, said: 'I saw your Prophet (during a time) when he was not able to even find low quality dates to fill his stomach.' (Muslim #2977)

Abu Hurairah, with whom Allah is pleased, said: 'The Messenger of Allah never filled his stomach for three consecutive days until his death.' (Bukhari #5059)

Even though the Arabian Peninsula was under his control, and he was the source of goodness for its people, the Prophet would at some times not find food to suffice him. His wife, A'ishah, with whom Allah is pleased, said that the Prophet bought some food from a Jew (and agreed to pay him at a later time) and he gave him his armor as collateral.' (Bukhari #2088)

This does not mean that he could not obtain what he wanted; for the moneys and wealth would be placed in front of him in his Masjid, and he would not move from his spot, until he distributed it amongst the poor and needy. Among his Companions were those who were wealthy and affluent - they would rush to serve him and would give up the most valuable of things for him. The reason the Prophet renounced the riches of this world, was because he knew the reality of this life.

He said: 'The likeness of this world to the Hereafter, is like a person who dipped his finger in the ocean - let him see what would return.' (Muslim #2858)

Reverend Bosworth Smith[20] said: ' - If ever a man ruled by a right divine, it was Muhammad, for he had all the powers without their supports. He cared not for the dressings of power. The simplicity of his private life was in keeping with his public life.'[21]

6. **Certain incidents would befall the Prophet of Allah** ﷺ **which would need clarification, and he would not be able to do anything because he did not receive revelation regarding it.** During this period (i.e. between the incident and revelation) he would be exhausted. One such incident is the incident of *Ifk*'[22] wherein the Prophet's wife A'ishah, with whom Allah is pleased, was accused of being treacherous. The Prophet ﷺ did not receive revelation concerning this incident for one month; during which his enemies talked ill of him, until revelation was revealed and the innocence of A'ishah was declared. Were the Prophet ﷺ an imposter he would have resolved this incident the minute it came about. Allah says:

⟨Nor does he speak out of desire.⟩ (53:3)

7. **The Prophet** ﷺ **did not ask people to adulate him.** On the contrary, the Prophet ﷺ would not be pleased if a person adulated him in any way. Anas, with whom Allah is pleased, said: 'There was no individual more beloved to the Companions than the Messenger of Allah.' He said: 'If they

---

[20] Encyclopedia of Seerah, by Afzalur-Rahman
[21] Muhammad and Muhammadanism
[22] i.e. The incident wherein the hypocrites falsely accused A'ishah, with whom Allah is pleased, of being unchaste.

---

saw him, they would not stand up for him, because they knew he disliked that.' (Tirmidthi #2754)

Washington Irving, said: 'His military triumphs awakened no pride nor vain glory as they would have done had they been effected by selfish purposes. In the time of his greatest power he maintained the same simplicity of manner and appearance as in the days of his adversity. So far from affecting regal state, he was displeased if, on entering a room, any unusual testimonial of respect was shown to him.'

8. **Some verses from the Qur'an were revealed in which the Prophet 🌺 was blamed and admonished,** due to some incident or happening; such as:

a. The words of Allah, the Exalted:

❨O Prophet! Why do you forbid (for yourself) that which Allah has allowed to you, seeking to please your wives? And Allah is Oft-Forgiving, Most Merciful.❩ (66:1)

The Prophet 🌺 abstained from eating honey, due to the behavior of some of his wives. Allah then admonished him because he forbade upon himself what Allah deemed lawful.

b. Allah, the Exalted, says:

❨May Allah forgive you (O Muhammad). Why did you grant them leave (for remaining behind; you should have persisted as regards your order to them to proceed on Jihad) until those who told the truth were seen by you in a clear light, and you had known the liars?❩ (9:43)

Allah admonished the Prophet 🌺 because he quickly accepted the false excuses of the hypocrites who lagged behind in the Battle of Tabuk. He forgave them and accepted their excuses, without verifying them.

c. Allah, the Exalted, says:

《It is not for a Prophet that he should have prisoners of war (and free them with ransom) until he had made a great slaughter (among his enemies) in the land. You desire the good of this world, but Allah desires for you the Hereafter. And Allah is All-Mighty, All-Wise.》 (8:67)

d. Allah, the Exalted, says:

《Not for you (O Muhammad, but for Allah) is the decision; whether He turns in mercy, to (pardon) them or punishes them; verily, they are the wrong-doers.》 (3:128)

e. Allah, the Exalted, says:

《The Prophet frowned and turned away. Because there came to him the blind man. And How can you know that he might become pure from sins? Or he might receive admonition, and the admonition might profit him?》 (80:1-4)

Abdullah b. Umm Maktoom, who was blind, came to the Prophet 🌸 while he was preaching to one or some of the Quraish leaders, and the Prophet 🌸 frowned and turned away - and Allah admonished him on account of that.

Therefore, were the Prophet 🌸 an imposter, these ayat would not be found in the Qur'an.

Muhammad Marmaduke Pickthall said: 'One day when the Prophet was in conversation with one of the great men of Qureysh, seeking to persuade him of the truth of Al-Islam, a blind man came and asked him a question concerning the faith. The Prophet was annoyed at the interruption, frowned and turned away from the blind man. In this Surah he is told that a man's importance is not to be judged from his appearance or worldly station.'[23]

9. **One of the sure signs of his Prophethood is found in the Chapter of *Lahab* (chapter 111) in the Qur'an.** In it Allah, the Exalted, condemned Abu Lahab (the Prophet's uncle) to the torment of Hell. This chapter was revealed during the early stages of his *Da'wah* (call to Islam). Were the Prophet 🕮 an imposter he would not issue a ruling like this; since his uncle might accept Islam afterwards!

Dr. Gary Miller says: 'For example, the Prophet 🕮 had an uncle by the name of Abu Lahab. This man hated Islam to such an extent that he used to follow the Prophet around in order to discredit him. If Abu Lahab saw the Prophet 🕮 speaking to a stranger, he would wait until they parted and then would go back to the stranger and ask him, 'What did he tell you? Did he say black? Well, it's white. Did he say 'Morning?' Well, it's night.' He faithfully said the exact opposite of whatever he heard Muhammad 🕮 say. However, about ten years before Abu Lahab died a little chapter in the Qur'an was revealed to him. It distinctly stated that he would go to the Fire (i.e. Hell). In other words, it affirmed that he would never become a Muslim and would therefore be condemned forever. For ten years all Abu Lahab had to do was say, 'I heard that it has been revealed to Muhammad that I will never change – that I will never become a Muslim and will enter the Hellfire. Well I want to become a Muslim now. How do you like that? What do you think of your divine revelation now?' But he never did that. And yet, that is exactly the kind of behavior one would have expected from him since he always sought to contradict Islam.

---

[23] The Glorious Qur'an pg. 685

In essence, Muhammad 🌸 said: 'You hate me and you want to finish me? Here, say these words, and I am finished. Come on, say them!' But Abu Lahab never said them. Ten years! And in all that time he never accepted Islam or even became sympathetic to the Islamic cause. How could Muhammad possibly have known for sure that Abu Lahab would fulfill the Qur'anic revelation if he (i.e. Muhammad) was not truly the Messenger of Allah? How could he possibly have been so confident as to give someone ten years to discredit his claim of Prophethood? The only answer is that he was Allah's Messenger; for in order to put forth such a risky challenge, one has to be entirely convinced that he has a divine revelation.'[24]

10. The Prophet 🌸 is called: 'Ahmed' in a verse of the Qur'an instead of 'Muhammad'. Allah, the Exalted, says:

❨And remember when Eesa, son of Maryam said: 'O Children of Israel! I am the Messenger of Allah unto you, confirming the Torah which came before me, and giving glad tidings of a Messenger to come after me, whose name shall be Ahmed. But when he came to them with clear proofs, they said: 'This is plain magic.'❩ (61:6)

Were he an imposter, the name 'Ahmed' would not have been mentioned in the Qur'an.

11. The *Deen* of Islam still exists today and is spreading all over the Globe. Thousands of people embrace Islam and prefer it over all other religions. This happens even though the callers to Islam are not financially backed as expected; and in spite of the efforts of the enemies of Islam to halt the spread of Islam. Allah, the Exalted, says:

---

[24] The Amazing Qur'an

❪Verily, We sent down the *Dhikr* (i.e. the Qur'an) and surely, We will guard it from corruption.❫ (15:9)

Thomas Carlyle said: 'A false man found a religion? Why, a false man cannot build a brick house! If he does not know and follow truly the properties of mortar, burnt clay and what else he works in, it is no house that he makes, but a rubbish-heap. It will not stand for twelve centuries, to lodge a hundred and eighty millions; it will fall straightway. A man must conform himself to Nature's laws, _be_ verily in communion with Nature and the truth of things, or Nature will answer him, No, not at all! Speciosities are specious--ah me!--a Cagliostro, many Cagliostros, prominent world-leaders, do prosper by their quackery, for a day. It is like a forged bank-note; they get it passed out of _their_ worthless hands: others, not they, have to smart for it. Nature bursts up in fire-flames; French Revolutions and such like, proclaiming with terrible veracity that forged notes are forged. But of a Great Man especially, of him I will venture to assert that it is incredible he should have been other than true. It seems to me the primary foundation of him, and of all that can lie in him, this.'[25]

The Prophet ﷺ preserved the Qur'an, after Allah had preserved it in the Books, chests of men generation after generation. Indeed memorizing and reciting it, learning and teaching it are among the things Muslims are very keen on doing, for the Prophet ﷺ said:

'The best of you are those who learn the Qur'an and teach it.' (Bukhari #4639)

---

[25] 'Heroes, Hero-Worship and the Heroic in History'

Many have tried to add and omit verses from the Qur'an, but they have never been successful; for these mistakes are discovered almost immediately.

As for the Sunnah of the Messenger of Allah 🕊 which is the second source of Shari'ah in Islam, it has been preserved by trustworthy pious men. They spent their lives gathering these traditions, and scrutinizing them to separate the weak from the authentic; they even clarified which narrations were fabricated. Whoever looks at the books written in the science of Hadeeth will realize this, and that the narrations that are authentic are in fact authentic.

Michael Hart[26] says: 'Muhammad founded and promulgated one of the world's great religions[27], and became an immensely effective political leader. Today, thirteen centuries after his death, his influence is still powerful and pervasive.'

12. **Veracity and truthfulness of his principles and that they are good and suitable for every time and place.** The results of the application of Islam are clear and well known, which in turn testify that it is indeed a revelation from Allah. Furthermore, why is it not possible for Prophet Muhammad 🕊 to be a Prophet - many Prophets and Messengers were sent before him. If the answer to this query is that there is nothing that prevents this - we then ask, 'why do you reject his Prophethood, and confirm the Prophethood of the Prophets before him?'

---

[26] 'The 100' A ranking of the most influential persons in history.
[27] We believe that Islam is a Divine revelation from Allah, and that Muhammad 🕊 did not found it.

13. **Man cannot bring about laws similar to the laws of Islam which deal with every aspect of life, such as transactions, marriage, social conduct, politics, acts of worship and the like.** So, how can an unlettered man bring something like this? Isn't this a clear proof and sign of his Prophethood?

14. **The Prophet ﷺ did not start calling people to Islam until he turned forty years old.** His youth had passed and the age in which he should have rest and spend his time leisurely, was the age in which he was commissioned as a Prophet and charged with the dissemination of Islam.

Thomas Carlyle, said: 'It goes greatly against the impostor theory, the fact that he lived in this entirely unexceptionable, entirely quiet and commonplace way, till the heat of his years was done. He was forty before he talked of any mission from Heaven. All his irregularities, real and supposed, date from after his fiftieth year, when the good Kadijah died. All his "ambition," seemingly, had been, hitherto, to live an honest life; his "fame," the mere good opinion of neighbors that knew him, had been sufficient hitherto. Not till he was already getting old, the prurient heat of his life all burnt out, and _peace_ growing to be the chief thing this world could give him, did he start on the "career of ambition;" and, belying all his past character and existence, set up as a wretched empty charlatan to acquire what he could now no longer enjoy! For my share, I have no faith whatever in that.'[28]

---

[28] 'Heroes, Hero-Worship and the Heroic in History'

What the Testimony of Faith *'There is no true god worthy of being worshipped except Allah and Muhammad is the Messenger of Allah'* entails:

1. To believe in the Message of the Prophet 鑭 and that he was sent to mankind at large; thus the Message of Islam is not restricted to a certain group of people or a period of time. Allah, the Exalted, says:

❨Blessed is He Who sent down the criterion to His slave that he may be a warner to mankind.❩ (25:1)

2. To believe that the Prophet 鑭 is infallible in matters pertaining to the *Deen*. Allah, the Exalted, says:

❨Nor does he speak of his own desire. It is only a revelation revealed.❩ (53:3-4)

As for worldly affairs, the Prophet 鑭 was only human and would make *Ijtihaad* (i.e. exert his effort to reach a ruling) in that matter.

The Prophet 鑭 said:

"You present your cases to me - some of you may be more eloquent and persuasive in presenting arguments than others. So, if I give someone's right to another (wrongly) because of the latter's (tricky) presentation of the case; I am giving him a piece of Fire; so he should not take it." (Agreed upon)[29]

He also said, in another narration:

---

[29] i.e. Both Imam Bukhari and Imam Muslim have narrated the Hadeeth in their collections through the same Companion.

"I am only human; opponents come to me to settle their problems. It may be that some of you can present his case more eloquently than the other - and I may consider him to be the rightful person and give a verdict in his favor. So, if I give the right of a Muslim to another by mistake, then it is only a portion of Hell-Fire, he has the option to take or give up before the Day of Resurrection." (Agreed Upon)

3. To believe that the Prophet 鏤 was sent as a mercy to mankind. Allah, the Exalted, says:

《And We have sent you not but as a mercy for mankind.》 (21:107)

Allah has certainly told the truth 《And who is truer in statement than Allah》 the Prophet 鏤 was a mercy to mankind. He delivered man from worshipping creatures, and guided them to worship the Creator of all creatures. He delivered man from the tyranny and injustices of (false and altered) religions to the justice and fairness of Islam. He delivered man from living a materialistic life to living a life wherein he works for the Hereafter.

4. To firmly believe that the Messenger of Allah 鏤 is the most honorable Prophet and Messenger, as well as the final Prophet and Messenger. No Prophet or Messenger will come after him. Allah, the Exalted, says:

《Muhammad is not the father of any of your men, but (he is) the Messenger of Allah, and the Last of the Prophets: and Allah has full knowledge of all things.》 (33:40)

The Prophet 鏤 said:

"I have been favored over all Prophets with six things: I have been given *Jawami al-Kalim*,[30] fear is instilled in the hearts of the enemy, booty and spoils of war have been made lawful for me, the whole earth is considered a place of prayer, and means of purification, and I was sent to mankind at large, and I am the final Prophet." (Muslim & Tirmidthi)

5. To firmly believe that the Prophet 🕮 conveyed to us the *Deen* of Islam, which is complete in all aspects. One cannot add something to the *Deen* nor can he omit something from it.

Allah, the Exalted, says:

❨This day, I have perfected your *Deen* for you, completed My favor upon you, and have chosen for you Islam as your *Deen*.❩ (5:3)

Islam is a complete way of life; it includes the social, political, economical and ethical aspects of life. It would lead one to live a prosperous life in this world and in the Hereafter.

Thomas Carlyle said: 'The Mahometans regard their Koran with a reverence which few Christians pay even to their Bible. It is admitted every where as the standard of all law and all practice; the thing to be gone upon in speculation and life; the message sent direct out of Heaven, which this Earth has to conform to, and walk by; the thing to be read. Their Judges decide by it; all Moslem are bound to study it, seek in it for the light of their life. They have mosques where it is all read daily; thirty relays of priests take it up in succession, get through the

---

[30] *Jawami al-Kalim* (conciseness of speech) is one of the miracles of the Prophet 🕮. The Prophet 🕮 would say a few words, and they would have great meanings.

whole each day. There, for twelve hundred years, has the voice of this Book, at all moments, kept sounding through the ears and the hearts of so many men. We hear of Mahometan Doctors that had read it seventy thousand times!'[31]

6. To firmly believe that the Messenger of Allah 🕮 conveyed the Message and gave sincere counseling to the *Ummah* (nation). There is no good except that he guided his Ummah to it, and there is no sinful act except that he warned people from it. The Prophet 🕮 said in the Farewell Pilgrimage:

> "Haven't I conveyed the Message of Allah to you?' They said, 'Yes (you have).' He said: 'O Allah! Bear witness!"
> (Agreed Upon)

7. To believe that the *Shari'ah* (Jurisprudential Law) of Muhammad 🕮 is the only acceptable *Shari'ah*. Mankind would be judged in light of this *Shari'ah*. Allah 🕮 says:

> ⟨And whoever seeks a *Deen* other than Islam, it will never be accepted of him, and in the Hereafter he will be one of the losers.⟩ (3:85)

8. To obey the Prophet 🕮. Allah, the Exalted, says:

> ⟨And whoever obeys Allah and the Messenger, these are with those upon whom Allah has bestowed favors from among the Prophets and the truthful and the martyrs and the good, and a goodly company they are!⟩ (4:69)

One obeys the Prophet 🕮 by obeying him and abstaining from what he prohibits.

---

[31] 'Heroes, Hero-Worship and the Heroic in History'

Allah, the Exalted, says:

❰And whatsoever the Messenger gives you, take it; and whatsoever he forbids you abstain from it.❱ (59:7)

Allah, the Exalted, clarified the punishment of him who does not refrain from what the Prophet 🕮 prohibited. He said:

❰And whosoever disobeys Allah and His Messenger, and transgresses His limits, He will cast him into the Fire, to abide therein; and he shall have a disgraceful torment.❱ (4:14)

9. To be content with the judgment of the Messenger of Allah 🕮 and to not demur what the Prophet 🕮 has legalized and made lawful. Allah, the Exalted, says:

❰Nay by your *Rubb*, they can have no faith, until they make you judge in all disputes between them, and find in themselves no resistance against your decisions, and accept with full submission.❱ (4:65)

Furthermore, one should not give precedence to anything over the *Shari'ah*. Allah 🕮 says:

❰Do they then seek the judgment of the Days of Ignorance? And who is better in judgment than Allah for a people who have firm faith.❱ (5:50)

10. To adhere to the Sunnah of the Prophet 🕮. Allah 🕮 says:

❰Say, 'if you really love Allah, then follow me, Allah will love you and forgive you your sins. And Allah is Oft-Forgiving, Most Merciful'.❱ (3:31)

One should emulate the Prophet 🕮 and take him as a supreme example. Allah 🕮 says:

❨Indeed in the Messenger of Allah you have a good example to follow for him who hopes for Allah and the Last Day, and remembers Allah much.❩ (33:21)

In order for one to emulate the Prophet 🌸 he has to learn and study the biography of the Prophet 🌸.

Zain al-Aabideen, may Allah have mercy on him, said: 'We were taught about the battles of the Messenger of Allah 🌸 as we were taught a verse from the Qur'an.'[32]

11. To hold the Prophet 🌸 in high esteem and to revere him. The Prophet 🌸 said:

'Do not over-adulate me for I was a slave of Allah before He commissioned me as a Messenger.' (At-Tabrani)

12. To ask Allah to exalt the mention of the Prophet 🌸. Allah says:

❨Indeed, Allah sends His Salah on the Prophet 🌸 and also His angels ask Allah to exalt his mention. O you who believe! Ask Allah to exalt the mention of the Prophet, and ask Allah to render the Prophet safe and secure from every derogatory thing.❩ (33:56)

The Prophet, may Allah exalt his mention, said:

'The miserly is him who upon hearing my name being mentioned does not ask Allah to exalt my mention.'

(Tirmidthi)

---

[32] Ibn Katheer, Al-Bidayah and al-Nihayah [The Beginning and the End] Vol. 3, p. 242

13. To love the Prophet 🕌 revere and respect him as he should be revered and respected; for humanity was guided to Islam through him. He should be revered and held more beloved to a person than his own self, for the one who accepts Islam would be prosperous in this life and in the Hereafter. Allah, the Exalted, says:

❲Say if your fathers, your sons, your brothers, your wives, your kindred, the wealth that you have gained, the commerce in which you fear a decline, and the dwellings in which you delight are dearer to you than Allah and His Messenger, and striving hard and fighting in His cause, then wait until Allah brings about His decision. And Allah guides not the people who are disobedient to Allah.❳ (9:24)

The Prophet 🕌 clarified the result of loving him; in his answer to the man who asked him: 'When is the Day of Resurrection?' The Prophet 🕌 said:

'What have you prepared for it?' The man did not answer immediately, and then said: 'O Messenger of Allah, I have not observed numerous (supererogatory) prayers, or fasts, or given charitable gifts, but I love Allah and His Messenger.' The Prophet 🕌 said: 'You will be summoned on the Day of Resurrection with whom you love!' (Bukhari & Muslim)

The Prophet 🕌 said:

'If man conceives three things, he will taste the sweetness and beauty of *Iman* (faith); (the first thing) that Allah and His Messenger are dearer to him than anything else, (the second thing) to love a person only for the sake of Allah, (the third thing) and to hate to return to *Kufr* (disbelief) after Allah delivers man from it, just as he hates to be cast into the Fire.' (Muslim)

Reverence and love of the Prophet 鱗 requires that a person love and revere whom he loved; such as his household, his Companions, with whom Allah is pleased. It also requires that a person abhor whom he abhorred, for the Prophet 鱗 loved and hated only for the sake of Allah.

14. To disseminate and invite people to Islam; and to revive the *Deen* of Allah, using wisdom and a good method. This is done by teaching the ignorant and reminding the one who is unaware, or has forgotten. Allah, the Exalted, says:

《Invite mankind to the way of your *Rubb* with wisdom and fair preaching, and argue with them in a way that is better.》 (16:125)

The Prophet 鱗 said:

'Convey from me, even one verse from the Qur'an.'

(Muslim)

15. To defend the Prophet 鱗 and his Sunnah, by refuting all fabricated narrations people have forged against him and clarifying all doubtful and dubious points raised by the enemies of Islam, and to spread the pure teachings of Islam to those who are ignorant of them.

16. To adhere to the Sunnah of the Prophet 鱗. He said:

'Adhere to my Sunnah and the Sunnah of the Rightly Guided Caliphs after me. Bite onto it with your molars[33],

---

[33] This is a parable, to express how keen a person should be in adhering to the Sunnah of the Messenger of Allah 鱗.

and stay away from all innovated matters. For every innovated matter (in matters of *Deen*) is a *Bid'ah*, and every *Bid'ah* is a means of misguidance.' (Bukhari & Muslim)

Conclusion

We conclude this research with the words of Alphonse de LaMartaine[34] in 'Historie de al Turquie':

'Never has a man set for himself, voluntarily or involuntarily, a more sublime aim, since this aim was superhuman; to subvert superstitions which had been imposed between man and his Creator, to render God unto man and man unto God; to restore the rational and sacred idea of divinity amidst the chaos of the material and disfigured gods of idolatry, then existing. Never has a man undertaken a work so far beyond human power with so feeble means, for he (Muhammad) had in the conception as well as in the execution of such a great design, no other instrument than himself and no other aid except a handful of men living in a corner of the desert. Finally, never has a man accomplished such a huge and lasting revolution in the world, because in less than two centuries after its appearance, Islam, in faith and in arms, reigned over the whole of Arabia, and conquered, in God's name, Persia Khorasan, Transoxania, Western India, Syria, Egypt, Abyssinia, all the known continent of Northern Africa, numerous islands of the Mediterranean Sea, Spain, and part of Gaul. "If greatness of purpose, smallness of means, and astonishing results are the three criteria of a human genius, who could dare compare any great man in history with Muhammad? The most famous men created arms, laws, and empires only. They founded, if anything at all, no more than material powers which often crumbled away before their eyes. This man moved not only armies, legislations, empires, peoples,

---

[34] He was a poet, a member of the provisional government, and a onetime presidential candidate. Here he recounts events in France in 1848.

dynasties, but millions of men in one-third of the then inhabited world; and more than that, he moved the altars, the gods, the religions, the ideas, the beliefs and the souls. "On the basis of a Book, every letter which has become law, he created a spiritual nationality which blends together peoples of every tongue and race. He has left the indelible characteristic of this Muslim nationality the hatred of false gods and the passion for the One and Immaterial God. This avenging patriotism against the profanation of Heaven formed the virtue of the followers of Muhammad; the conquest of one-third the earth to the dogma was his miracle; or rather it was not the miracle of man but that of reason. "The idea of the unity of God, proclaimed amidst the exhaustion of the fabulous theogonies, was in itself such a miracle that upon it's utterance from his lips it destroyed all the ancient temples of idols and set on fire one-third of the world. His life, his meditations, his heroic reveling against the superstitions of his country, and his boldness in defying the furies of idolatry, his firmness in enduring them for fifteen years in Mecca, his acceptance of the role of public scorn and almost of being a victim of his fellow countrymen: all these and finally, his flight, his incessant preaching, his wars against odds, his faith in his success and his superhuman security in misfortune, his forbearance in victory, his ambition, which was entirely devoted to one idea and in no manner striving for an empire; his endless prayers, his mystic conversations with God, his death and his triumph after death; all these attest not to an imposture but to a firm conviction which gave him the power to restore a dogma. This dogma was twofold the unity of God and the immateriality of God: the former telling what God is, the latter telling what God is not; the one overthrowing false gods with the sword, the other starting an idea with words.

"Philosopher, Orator, Apostle, Legislator, Conqueror of Ideas, Restorer of Rational beliefs....The founder of twenty terrestrial empires and of one spiritual empire that is Muhammad. As regards all standards by which human greatness may be measured, we may well ask, is there any man greater than he?'

الحمد لله رب العالمين

وصلى الله وسلم على نبينا محمد وآله وسلم

All Praise is due to Allah alone, the *Rubb* of the Worlds

And may Allah exalt the mention of His Prophet and his household and render him safe from every derogatory thing

If you would like to receive more information about Islam, do not hesitate to contact us:

1) Email:

en@islamland.org

2) You may also visit the following sites:

http://www.islamland.org   http://www.sultan.org
http://www.islamtoday.com   www.islam-guide.com
http://www.daralmadinah.com   www.islamhouse.com
http://www.islamworld.net   www.islamhouse.tv

Glossary

1. Aqeedah: Creed.

3. Dinar & Dirham: A type of money.

4. Fareedhah: An obligatory act of worship.

5. Fitnah: Trial, strife and tribulation.

6. Hadeeth: Prophetic Tradition.

7. Hawdh: The Pool which Allah, the Exalted, has granted our Prophet 🙲 on the Day of Resurrection. Whoever drinks from it once, would never feel thirsty again.

8. Hudood: Castigatory punishments in Islam.

9. Hukum: Ruling.

10. Ijtihaad: In general, it is the exertion of effort. In this book it refers to exertion of one's effort to reach a ruling in an issue.

11. I'tikaaf: In general, it refers to seclusion. *I'tikaaf* is an act of worship whereby the person secludes himself in the Masjid and worships Allah.

12. Iman: Belief.

13. Jannah: This is the Heavenly Abode or Heavenly Gardens which Allah grants the pious slaves in the Hereafter. It is mistranslated as 'Paradise'.

14. Jawami al-Kalim: (conciseness of speech) is one of the miracles of the Prophet 🙲. The Prophet 🙲 would say a few words, and they would have great meanings.

15. Kufr: Disbelief.

16. Nafl: Supererogatory acts of worship.

17. Shaitan: Satan.

18. Shari'ah: Islamic Jurisprudential Law.

19. Shirk: Associating partners with Allah.

20. Sunnah: Has more than one meaning. It may refer to:

a. Prophetic Traditions.

b. Rulings; i.e. it would then mean that the act is endorsed by the *Sunnah*.

21. Taqwah: Piety.

22. Ummah: Nation.

23. Wali: The pious, god-fearing, upright Muslim, who is mindful of Allah, observes acts of worship, and abstains from the unlawful.

Table of Contents

http://www.islamhouse.com